TAXATION OF
S CORPORATIONS
IN A NUTSHELL

By

DOUGLAS A. KAHN
Paul G. Kauper Professor of Law
University of Michigan Law School

JEFFREY H. KAHN
Professor of Law
The Pennsylvania State University
Dickinson School of Law

TERRENCE G. PERRIS
Partner
Squire, Sanders & Dempsey L.L.P.

THOMSON
WEST

Mat #40657429

© 2008 Thomson/West
      610 Opperman Drive
      St. Paul, MN 55123
      1–800–313–9378

Printed in the United States of America

ISBN: 978–0–314–18492–4

TEXT IS PRINTED ON 10% POST
CONSUMER RECYCLED PAPER

To my brother, Edwin, who was the inspiration for my professional career.

—DAK

Cui dono lepidum novum libellum?
To Professors Kahn, Perris and Newton, three truly amazing professors.

—JHK

To the memory of my grandfather, George A. Sfakianos, who made it all possible.

—TGP

*

PREFACE

S corporations are a popular form of conducting business, especially for small business operations. They combine the advantages of a corporate structure, including access to the nonrecognition tax provisions that apply to certain combinations of corporate entities, with the pass-through of tax attributes that partnerships provide. With the rise of the Limited Liability Company (LLC) form of conducting business, many predicted that the use of S corporations would shrink as most small businesses would choose the LLC form. Contrary to those expectations, while the LLC has proved to be a popular vehicle, the use of S corporations has continued to thrive. In 2006, over 3.8 million returns were filed by S corporations. That number represents a 5.2 percent increase from 2005 and almost 1.4 million more returns than those filed by C corporations.

The S corporation was introduced in 1958 when Congress added Subchapter S to the Code. As originally adopted, it was available only to closely held corporations (the number of permissible shareholders was limited to ten, and the types of persons who were permitted to hold stock of an S corporation were severely restricted), and its pass-through treatment of tax items was narrower than that of partnerships. The scope of the Subchapter S provisions has been expanded over the years. An S corporation can now have as many as one hundred shareholders, and it can have even more than that because of the liberal treatment of a broad range of family members as a single shareholder for purposes of the 100-shareholder limit. The types of persons who are permitted to hold stock in an S corporation also have been expanded. The pass-through treatment of tax items to an S corporation's shareholders has become much more similar to the manner in which partnership tax items pass through to the partners. Now, all tax items pass through to the shareholders and have the same character in the hands of the shareholders as the item had for the corporation.

Anyone who plans to engage in advising closely held businesses needs to have an understanding of the requirements and operation of the Subchapter S provisions in order to be able to compare the relative advantages and disadvantages of each form that is available for conducting a specific business. The S corporation's application of a pass-through system may induce a deceptive inference that the provisions are relatively simple to apply. Unfortunately, that is not the case.

The goal of this book is to provide the reader with a foundation in the basic structure of Subchapter S. We do examine some of its details so that the reader will be better able to understand the benefits and costs of conducting business in this form. We also discuss the historical background of some provisions to provide the reader with a fuller understanding of the current provisions and what problems they were designed to cure. We have not attempted to cover every aspect of Subchapter S. That would require a multi-volume treatise. We have, however, covered all of the material that is likely to be included in a law school course on this subject.

The book is designed primarily for a law student and for those who are unfamiliar with the manner in which Subchapter S operates. Numerous examples are included in order to illustrate the principles discussed and to help the reader understand how they operate. Our goal is to provide a clear explanation of a complex set of rules and to place them into perspective by showing the problems they are designed to reach.

The organization of the book begins with an examination of the requirements that a corporation must meet in order to qualify to make an election to be an S corporation. This includes an examination of the types and number of shareholders that are permitted. The manner and timing of an election and the date on which a valid election becomes effective are explained. The book then addresses the tax treatment accorded to an S corporation and its shareholders. This part includes the pass through of the corporation's tax items, the extent to which shareholders can deduct pass-through losses, the carryover of deductions that a shareholder cannot utilize in a taxable year, and the treatment of distributions from a corporation to a shareholder both while the corporation is still an S corporation and afterwards. The book then examines how an election for Subchapter S treatment can be terminated—voluntarily or involuntarily. The book examines the consequences of a termination of an election, especially when the termination occurs during a taxable year (as contrasted to a termination occurring on the first day of a taxable year). Lastly, the book examines the circumstances in which an S corporation pays tax on any of its income and the manner in which the taxation of an S corporation's income operates.

The authors would like to thank Idan Netser for his assistance in preparing the index.

DOUGLAS A. KAHN
JEFFREY H. KAHN
TERRENCE G. PERRIS

September 15, 2007

OUTLINE

TABLE OF CASES

References are to Pages

*

TABLE OF STATUTES

UNITED STATES

UNITED STATES CODE ANNOTATED
26 U.S.C.A.—Internal Revenue Code

TABLE OF STATUTES

UNITED STATES CODE ANNOTATED
26 U.S.C.A.—Internal Revenue Code

TABLE OF STATUTES

UNITED STATES CODE ANNOTATED
26 U.S.C.A.—Internal Revenue Code

TABLE OF STATUTES

UNITED STATES CODE ANNOTATED
26 U.S.C.A.—Internal Revenue Code

XVIII

TABLE OF STATUTES

UNITED STATES CODE ANNOTATED
26 U.S.C.A.—Internal Revenue Code

UNITED STATES CODE ANNOTATED
26 U.S.C.A.—Internal Revenue Code

UNITED STATES CODE ANNOTATED
26 U.S.C.A.—Internal Revenue Code

UNITED STATES CODE ANNOTATED
26 U.S.C.A.—Internal Revenue Code

UNITED STATES CODE ANNOTATED
26 U.S.C.A.—Internal Revenue Code

UNITED STATES CODE ANNOTATED
26 U.S.C.A.—Internal Revenue Code

UNITED STATES CODE ANNOTATED
26 U.S.C.A.—Internal Revenue Code

UNITED STATES CODE ANNOTATED
26 U.S.C.A.—Internal Revenue Code

TABLE OF STATUTES

UNITED STATES CODE ANNOTATED
26 U.S.C.A.—Internal Revenue Code

*

TABLE OF REGULATIONS

TABLE OF REGULATIONS

TREASURY REGULATIONS

TABLE OF REGULATIONS

TREASURY REGULATIONS

TABLE OF REGULATIONS

TREASURY REGULATIONS

REVENUE PROCEDURES

REVENUE RULINGS

TABLE OF REGULATIONS

REVENUE RULINGS

PRIVATE LETTER RULINGS

GENERAL COUNCIL MEMORANDUM

TECHNICAL ADVICE MEMORANDUM

*

TAXATION OF
S CORPORATIONS

IN A NUTSHELL

*

CHAPTER 1

INTRODUCTION

§ 1. Special Treatment of Closely Held Corporations

Generally, our current tax system treats a corporation as a tax-paying entity that is separate and distinct from its shareholders and imposes a double tax on corporate earnings that are distributed to the shareholders. On the other hand, most partnerships are treated as a pass-through entity for which only one tax is imposed. One consequence of this conflicting treatment is that the determination of whether to conduct a business venture in corporate form or in the form of a partnership, Limited Liability Company (LLC), or a sole proprietorship will be influenced by the differences in the federal income tax treatment applied to those business forms. A Limited Liability Company (LLC) and a Limited Liability Partnership (LLP) are unincorporated organizations that can be taxed, at their election, either as a corporation or as a partnership if the organization has more than one member. If the organization has only one member, either it can be taxed as a corporation or it can be disregarded as an entity for tax purposes. Treas. Reg. § 301.7701–3. The influence of tax considerations in choosing a business form is most pronounced for small, closely held business ventures since the nontax benefits of incorporating are often less significant for small, closely held operations than for the large, publicly held ventures.

In 1958, responding to a concern for stimulating small business ventures, Congress adopted several provisions to *mitigate* (but not to eliminate) the disadvantageous differences in tax treatment accorded to corporations on the one hand and to partnerships and sole proprietorships on the other. The most important of those provisions was the addition to the Code of Subchapter S. The provisions of Subchapter S were substantially altered by the adoption of the Subchapter S Revision Act of 1982 and by the Small Business Job Protection Act of 1996 and have been further amended, on a modest scale, by legislation enacted from time to time.

Subchapter S permits certain relatively small corporations to elect not to be taxed on most or all of their income and, instead, to have their income, deductions and credits allocated to their shareholders. The reference to "small" corporations refers to the number of shareholders the corporation has; the size of the corporation's net worth and gross receipts is of no consequence in determining whether the corporation qualifies. Thus, the S corporation form can be available for very large businesses that are already in corporate form and desire to escape the burden of the double tax regime that is a prime element of Subchapter C of the Code, which governs the taxation of corporations other than S corporations. For example, some public companies with a relatively small number of public shareholders have made the decision to "go private" through leveraged buy-out transactions and then, with the benefit of the resulting reduced number of shareholders, to elect to be an S corporation.

The availability of Subchapter S treatment has been expanded by the amendments made to that provision. For example, when initially adopted in 1958, the maximum number of shareholders that an S corporation could have was 10; currently, that number has been raised to 100. As we will see, the number can substantially exceed 100 if stock is held by multiple members of one or more families.

Unless indicated otherwise, any citation to a "§" number in this book is to the Internal Revenue Code of 1986, as amended. If reference is made to a section of a chapter of this book, the word "section" will be spelled out.

In 1958, Congress also adopted § 1244 to provide, in certain prescribed circumstances, ordinary loss treatment (instead of the capital loss treatment that otherwise would apply) for losses incurred by an individual shareholder on "small business stock," subject to dollar limitations as to the amount of loss that can qualify.

In 1993, Congress provided special relief for gain recognized from the sale or exchange of "qualified small business stock" as defined in § 1202(c). If this treatment is applicable, generally only 50% of the gain from the disposition of such stock is included in gross income; but a different percentage can apply because of dollar limitations on the amount that can be excluded and because a higher percentage of the gain is excluded for a specified category of businesses. However, there is a higher capital gain rate on the gain remaining after excluding the § 1202 amount than is imposed on most capital gains. § 1(h)(1)(E), (3), (4), (7). In general, the included gain will be taxed at a 28% rate unless the taxpayer's marginal ordinary income tax rate is lower.

§ 2. General Explanation of Subchapter S

The reference to Subchapter S is to Subchapter S of Chapter 1 of Subtitle A of Title 26 of the United States Code. The provisions of Subchapter S, which are set forth in §§ 1361–1379, apply to a corporation only if both the corporation and all of its shareholders make a valid election, and then only if the corporation qualifies for that treatment. The requirements for making a valid election and for the corporation's qualifying for the treatment are described later in this book.

A corporation for which a valid election for Subchapter S treatment is effective is commonly referred to as an "S corporation." Any corporation that is not an S corporation is referred to as a "C corporation." § 1361(a). The name "C corporation" reflects the fact that Subchapter C includes the principal tax provisions that control the treatment of those corporations. While many of the provisions of Subchapter C also apply to S corporations, the latter are subject to Subchapter S provisions as well.

Subject to four exceptions, one of which is virtually obsolete, a corporation for which a valid Subchapter S election has been made will pay no federal income tax. The four exceptions that require an S corporation to pay an income tax in certain circumstances do not apply to a corporation that has been an S corporation since its inception and has not obtained from a C corporation, in a nonrecognition transaction, an asset that was appreciated in value at the time of the transfer to the S corporation. § 1374(c)(1), (d)(8)(B)(ii). The four exceptions are discussed later in this chapter.

The following is a very general description of the workings of Subchapter S. A more detailed explanation is set forth in subsequent chapters of this book.

The purpose of Subchapter S is to prevent the double taxation of corporate income for certain qualified and electing corporations. An S corporation generally does not pay taxes on its income. Instead, the income and other tax items of an S corporation, as determined at the end of its taxable year, pass through to its shareholders in proportion to their stock holdings. In general, the shareholders will increase the basis in their corporate stock for income that passes through to them, and they will reduce their basis in the corporation's stock for losses or deductions that pass through to them. Since the corporation's income is taxed to its shareholders at the end of the corporation's taxable year, even when not distributed to the shareholders, an S corporation's distribution to a shareholder generally does not cause the shareholder to recognize income. Instead, the shareholder reduces his basis in his corporate stock. If the distribution exceeds the shareholder's basis, the excess is treated as a gain from the sale of the stock. § 1368(b). If an S corporation has earnings and profits, which can occur either because the corporation previously had been a C corporation or because the corporation is a successor to a C corporation, a distribution can be a dividend. See Chapter 6.

In effect, a shareholder's basis in his stock is increased when the corporation earns income, and then is reduced when the income is distributed to the shareholder. In this respect, the Code treats S corporation shareholders similarly to the partners of a partnership. This treatment assures that the corporation's income will be taxed only once, and that tax will be paid by the shareholders. There are certain circumstances in which a shareholder can be taxed on an S corporation's distribution to him, and those circumstances are described and explained in Chapter 6.

The four exceptions to an S corporation's exclusion from income tax liability, which are described more fully later in this book, are that in certain circumstances an S corporation:

(1) may be taxed on the amount of its recognized gains that is attributable to appreciation that previously occurred (or to income previously earned) in the hands of a C corporation,

(2) may be taxed on a portion of its passive investment income,

(3) will pay the tax caused by a recapture of an investment credit that was taken in a prior year in which the corporation was a C corporation (as a consequence of the substantial reduction of the scope of the investment tax credit by the 1986 TRA, this third exception is of little or no significance.),

(4) will pay the tax (in four installments) on the LIFO recapture amount that the corporation recognized in the last year that it was a C corporation. This fourth exception is actually a tax imposed on the corporation while it was still a C corporation, but it is payable by the corporation after it became an S corporation. The LIFO recapture amount provision is described in more detail later in the book. See Section 2(g) of Chapter 9.

Subject to the four exceptions noted above, the tax items of an S corporation (such as long-term and short-term capital gains and losses, section 1231 gains and losses, ordinary income and losses, tax-exempt income, charitable contributions, deductions and credits) are not taxed to the corporation but rather are passed through and allocated among the shareholders proportionately to their stock holdings; and the shareholders report those allocated items as if they recognized them directly. As we will see, an S corporation is permitted to have only one class of stock; and so the proportional allocation of the corporation's tax items is easy to calculate.

Even income that is taxed to the S corporation under one of the exceptions will pass through to the shareholders and be taxed again in their hands. However, the amount that passes through to the shareholders effectively will be reduced by the tax that the S corporation incurred. § 1366(f)(2), (3).

Prior to the adoption of the Subchapter S Revision Act of 1982 (hereinafter referred to as the "SRA"), only a few of the tax items of an S corporation were passed through to the shareholders (for example, there was no pass through of the corporation's capital losses in excess of its capital gains), and all corporate income that was passed through to a shareholder was treated either as ordinary dividend income or as a long-term capital gain. The SRA changed this feature of an S corporation, and made many other important changes in the treatment of S corporations and their shareholders. Tax items of an S corporation now pass through to its shareholders with the same character that the items had to the corporation. A shareholder's basis in his stock of an S corporation is adjusted to reflect many of the corporation's tax items that pass through to the shareholder.

It is sometimes said that an S corporation is a corporation that has elected to be taxed as a partnership. That overstates the tax similarities shared by partnerships and S corporations. While the several amendments that have been made over the years to Subchapter S have substantially reduced the differences in the tax treatment of S corporations and partnerships, significant differences remain. Later in this book, when we explain the operation of Subchapter S in greater detail, we will point out some of those differences.

§ 3. Application of Subchapter C to S Corporations

As previously noted, a corporation for which a valid election under Subchapter S is in effect is referred to as an "S corporation"; and any corporation that is not an S corporation is referred to as a "C corporation." This terminology is not limited to the provisions of Subchapter S itself; it also is utilized in various provisions of the Code outside Subchapter S. See, e.g., §§ 56(g)(6), 59(e)(4)(C), 108(d)(7), 179(d)(8), 267(b)(11), (12), 318(a)(5)(E).

Unless provided otherwise in Subchapter S or elsewhere in the Code, or unless inconsistent with the terms of Subchapter S, the provisions of Subchapter C are applied to an S corporation in the same manner as they apply to any other corporation. § 1371(a). However, the Code does prescribe numerous differences. For example, subject to a number of exceptions, the taxable income of an S corporation is computed in the same manner as is applied to individuals. § 1363(b). Thus, the dividend-received deduction provided by § 243(a) for dividends received by corporate shareholders is not available to S corporations. Of the numerous statutory provisions that treat S corporations differently from C corporations, some treat an

S corporation the same as an individual; some treat it as a partnership; and some treat it as a so-called "pass-thru" entity. See, e.g., §§ 1372(a), 1373(a), 267(e)(2), 67(c), Treas. Reg. § 1.67–2T(g)(1)(iii).

The provision in § 1363(b) that, subject to exceptions, an S corporation's taxable income is to be determined the same as that of an individual does not prevent the application of Subchapter C to S corporations. One obvious purpose of § 1363(b) is to insure that dividends paid to an S corporation will not qualify for the special deduction accorded to corporate shareholders. There is no intention to deny an S corporation the benefits of nonrecognition or other provisions in which the absence of a corporate level tax would not conflict with the purpose for providing those benefits.

There are numerous examples in which the provisions of Subchapter C have been applied to S corporations. Thus, the reorganization provisions (including nonrecognition of gain or loss) apply to S corporations. GCM 39768. Also, in TAM 9245004, reversing his prior position, the Commissioner held that an S corporation qualifies to make a valid § 338 election for a target whose stock the S corporation had acquired in a qualified stock purchase. The reader will recall that a § 338 election is available only when a *corporation* makes a qualified stock purchase of a target corporation's stock. § 338(a). In that TAM, the Commissioner also ruled that the S corporation's subsequent liquidation of the target qualified as a § 332 liquidation (a nonrecognition provision for liquidations of a controlled subsidiary corporation). In addition, a corporation purchasing the stock of an S corporation is permitted to join with the shareholders of the S corporation in making an election under § 338(h)(10) to recharacterize the transaction as a purchase of the S corporation's assets followed by a liquidation of the S corporation. Treas. Reg. § 1.338(h)(10)–1(c)(1).

Considerable care should be taken in determining how other Code provisions apply to S corporations. One illustration is the operation of the stock attribution rules of § 318. For purposes of attributing stock held by an S corporation to its shareholders or vice versa, § 318(a)(5)(E) treats the S corporation as a partnership and treats its shareholders as partners. Consequently, attribution to or from a shareholder of an S corporation is not subject to the 50 percent stock holding requirement applied to C corporations and their shareholders by § 318(a)(2)(C), (3)(C). However, for other purposes, § 318(a)(5)(E) treats an S corporation as a corporation. As a result, the outstanding stock of an S corporation is subject to the § 318 stock attribution rules, whereas an interest in a partnership is not.

CHAPTER 2

ELIGIBILITY TO QUALIFY AS AN S CORPORATION

§ 1. In General

To qualify for Subchapter S treatment, an electing corporation must satisfy the requirements set forth in § 1361. A corporation that qualifies to elect Subchapter S treatment is referred to as a "small business corporation." Note that a "small business corporation" is one that meets the qualifications to make a Subchapter S election, but it will not be an S corporation unless a valid election is made. The "small" in that term refers to the number of shareholders that an S corporation is permitted to have; there are no limitations on the size of an S corporation's net worth or on the amount of its income. A corporation must satisfy the following requirements to be a "small business corporation."(§ 1361(b)).

(1) It must be a domestic corporation.

(2) It must not be one of four types of corporations that are declared to be ineligible for Subchapter S treatment by § 1361(b)(2). An example of an "ineligi-

ble corporation" is an insurance company subject to tax under Subchapter L.

(3) It must not have a nonresident alien as a shareholder.

(4) It must not have more than one class of stock.

(5) It must not have a shareholder who is neither an individual, nor an estate, nor a type of trust described in § 1361(c)(2) or (d), nor a tax exempt organization described in § 1361(c)(6). The types of trusts that are permitted to be shareholders of an S corporation are described in Section 3 of this chapter. The types of "estates" that are permitted to hold stock in an S corporation are a decedent's estate and the estate of a bankrupt individual. If the corporation's stock is held by the estate of a decedent, it is the estate that is treated as the shareholder, and not the beneficiaries of the estate. Treas. Reg. § 1.1361–1(e)(1). Thus, the estate counts as one shareholder, and a beneficiary of the estate can be a person who is not qualified to hold an S Corporation's stock. In contrast, a trust typically is not treated as the shareholder.

An S corporation is permitted to be a subsidiary of another S corporation if certain conditions (described in Section 2 of this chapter) are satisfied. Such a subsidiary is referred to as a "Qualified Subchapter S Subsidiary" (QSSS), which is often referred to in practice and in the regulations as a "QSub." In all other respects, a corporation—even an S corporation—is not a permitted shareholder of an S corporation. Interestingly, an S corporation may be a stockholder of another corporation without disqualifying its S election, but its S election will be disqualified if another corporation acquires the S corporation's stock (subject to the potential of a QSub election if the other corporation acquires all of the S corporation's stock). In addition, while an S corporation may be a member of a partnership, its S election will be terminated if a partnership acquires any stock of the S corporation.

At times, we refer in this material to a person (such as a C corporation) that is not permitted to hold stock in an S corporation. Of course, the person is not prohibited from holding the stock; rather, this reference means that the person's holding of stock disqualifies the corporation for Subchapter S treatment.

(6) It must have no more than 100 shareholders. In counting the number of a corporation's shareholders, stock held by spouses and their estates is treated as

stock held by only one shareholder. § 1361(c)(1)(A)(i). For this purpose, it does not matter whether the stock is held by the spouses (or an estate of a spouse) individually or in some form of joint ownership. This spousal provision was made redundant by the family members provision described below.

In counting the number of shareholders, all "members of a family" and their estates are treated as only one shareholder. § 1361(c)(1)(A)(ii). The members of a family are defined to refer to a common ancestor, all lineal descendants of that ancestor, and the spouses and former spouses of the common ancestor and the lineal descendants. The generation spread between the common ancestor and the youngest generation of the ancestor's "family" who hold stock in the corporation cannot exceed six generations at the later of the earliest time that a member of the family acquires stock in the S corporation or at the time that the subchapter S election was made, or at the date, October 22, 2004. § 1361(c)(1)(B). The "members of a family" provision was added to the Code in 2004 and modified in 2005.

The scope of the "members of a family" provision is extraordinarily broad. For example, consider how the family of K, who is a shareholder of the X corporation, can be determined under the statute. K is married to $W2$, and is divorced from $W1$. Neither $W1$ nor $W2$ owns any stock of X. There are a number of alternative methods for determining the identity of the other shareholders of X who can be combined with K to be treated as a single shareholder.

One available approach is to go back six generations from K and select one of K's ancestors in that generation. If that ancestor has a family member who is of a younger generation than K and is a shareholder, then one cannot use that ancestor, but must use an ancestor that is no more than six generations removed from the youngest generation family member who is also a shareholder. Once the ancestor is identified, that ancestor, his or her spouse and former spouse, and all of that ancestor's lineal descendants and their spouses and former spouses are members of the same family and count as one shareholder. In addition, the estate of a deceased member of that group is included in the group that is treated as one shareholder.

Obviously, there are numerous ancestors that could be utilized as the source of a family whose members are to be combined. Presumably, the ancestor that will be utilized as the source will be the one who provides the optimal result in minimizing the number of shareholders who are counted in applying the 100–shareholder limit.

In the example above, if it combines a larger number of shareholders, it is possible (but not certain) that one could utilize as the source of a family an ancestor of either *W2* or *W1* (subject to the six generation separation limitation), and then the lineal descendants of that ancestor and their spouses and former spouses would be treated as one shareholder. If so, *K* would be a member of that family.

It is an open question whether the "common ancestor" referred to in § 1361(c)(1)(B)(i) applies only to an ancestor of a *shareholder* or whether it can also apply to an ancestor of a spouse or former spouse of a shareholder. The statute treats "members of a family" as one shareholder and then defines the members of a family as a common ancestor, lineal descendants, spouses and former spouses thereof. If a spouse or former spouse of a lineal descendant of *A* is a shareholder, that shareholder would be a member of *A*'s family; and so it seems that *A* can qualify as a common ancestor of a family even though no lineal descendant of *A* owns stock of the corporation. Not only has this issue not been resolved, it has not even been addressed.

Section 1361(c)(1)(B)(ii) states that an individual cannot qualify as a common ancestor if "the individual is more than six generations removed from the youngest *generation of shareholders* who would (but for this subparagraph) be members of the family" (Emphasis added). The statute then states that a spouse or former spouse is treated as being of the same generation as the individual to whom that spouse is (or was) married. It seems to the authors that this provision limits the choice of an ancestor to one who is no more than six generations removed from the youngest generation of shareholders who are members of the ancestor's family within the statutory definition of that term. In other words, the limitation refers to a generation in which one or more members of the ancestor's family are shareholders, but it does not require that the member of the family who is a shareholder be a descendant of the chosen ancestor. As noted, this issue is unresolved.

If *W1* or *W2* owns stock of *X*, then it is much clearer that an ancestor of that person could be utilized, and *K* would then qualify as a member of that family as a spouse or former spouse of a descendant of the ancestor. If it is crucial to Subchapter S qualification that a common ancestor of *W1* or *W2* be utilized as the source of the family to be combined, *K* could make a bona fide gift of a share of X stock to *W1* or *W2* to avoid that issue. It is important that the gift be bona fide and not a sham arrangement.

As we have noted above, the statute clearly requires that the generation spread between the common ancestor and the youngest family member owning stock of the S corporation cannot exceed six generations. However, as expressly stated in the proposed regulations, "the [six-generation] test is only applied at the applicable date, and lineal descendants (and spouses) more than six generations removed from the common ancestor will be treated as members of the family even if they acquire stock of the corporation after that date." Prop. Reg. § 1.1361–1(e)(3)(*l*) (September 27, 2007). See also, Douglas A. Kahn, Jeffrey H. Kahn and Terrence G. Perris, "All in the Family as a Single Shareholder of an S Corporation," 116 Tax Notes 791 (August 27, 2007). Subsequent to October

22, 2004, the applicable date is the later of the date on which the first family member acquired stock of the S corporation or the date on which the S corporation election was made. § 1361(c)(1)(B)(iii).

A 2007 amendment added § 1361(f) to the Code. That amendment provides special treatment for certain stock of a corporation that is a bank. This special type of stock is referred to as "restricted bank director stock." In general, this refers to stock held by a director of a bank who is required by federal or state law to hold that stock in order to be eligible to serve as a director. Another requirement is that there must be a contractual obligation for the shareholder to sell the stock back to the bank or to its parent corporation in the event that the shareholder ceases to be a director of the bank. Restricted bank director stock is not treated as stock for most tax purposes; and so the holder of that stock is not thereby treated as a shareholder in determining whether the corporation complies with the restricted number of shareholders; and the stock will not be treated as a second class of stock. Distributions to the director that are made with respect to that stock (other than distributions in exchange for the stock) are not treated as distributions to a shareholder, but rather are treated as compensation paid to the director that is deductible by the corporation and included in the gross income of the director.

If more than 100 persons wish to form an S corporation, they can accomplish a similar result by forming two or more S corporations each of which has separate shareholders and does not violate the shareholder limitation. The several S corporations can then form a partnership to operate the business. Under partnership taxation (Subchapter K), the income of the business will be allocated among the several S corporations and then, in turn allocated among the shareholders of each corporation under Subchapter S rules. Reversing its prior position, the Service agreed in Rev. Rul. 94–43 that such an arrangement does not violate the shareholder limitation rule. With the substantial expansion of the number of persons who can be S corporation shareholders since this revenue ruling was published, it is less likely that this partnership structure will be needed to deal with the shareholder limit. However, it seems likely that such a partnership form can be utilized to avoid other restrictions on Subchapter S as well. For example, Treas. Reg. § 1.701–2(d), Ex. (2) indicates that an S corporation can form a partnership with a nonresident alien in order to avoid the prohibition against an S corporation's having a shareholder who is a nonresident alien.

Ex. (1) The X Corporation has 3,050 shares of voting common stock outstanding. X has only one class of stock outstanding. Except for the 100–shareholder limitation, X satisfies all the other requirements for qualifying as an S corporation. Each of 99 unrelated individuals owns 30 shares of X's stock (totaling 2,970 shares), which stock is held in the single name of the individual who holds his respective 30 shares. The remaining 80 shares of X's stock are held by A and B as joint tenants with rights of survivorship. While A and B are unrelated to each other and to any of the other 99 shareholders, they have lived together as partners for many years. A and B are each treated as a separate shareholder even though they hold their stock in joint tenancy. Therefore, X will not qualify as an S corporation since it has 101 shareholders—one more than the permitted number.

Ex. (2) The same facts as those stated in **Ex. (1)** except that A and B are husband and wife. For purposes of counting the number of X's shareholders, a husband and wife are treated as only one shareholder. Since A and B are counted as only one shareholder, X does qualify as an S corporation. The result would be the same if A and B held their 80 shares of X's stock as tenants in common rather than as joint tenants. Indeed, it would not matter if they did not hold the 80 shares as co-tenants; but, instead, A held 30 shares of X's stock in his individual name and B held 50 shares of X's stock in her individual name. Even in that case, A and B would be counted as only one shareholder.

Ex. (3) The same facts as those stated in **Ex. (1)** except that A and B are husband and wife, and A holds 30 shares of X's stock in his individual name, and B holds 50 shares of X's stock in her individual name. As noted in **Ex. (2)**, so long as A and B are married, they are treated as a single shareholder; and so X qualifies as an S corporation.

Four years after acquiring their X stock, A and B are divorced, and they continue to hold their shares of X stock in their individual names. Prior to the 2004 and 2005 amendments adding the provision that makes "members of a family" count as one shareholder, the divorce would have caused A and B to be counted as two shareholders immediately after it became final. However, under the current rules, each of the parties would then be the former spouse of a lineal descendant of a common ancestor of the other spouse and so A and B will continue to be treated as one shareholder. X will continue to qualify as an S corporation.

Ex. (4) The same facts as those stated in **Ex. (1)** except that A and B are husband and wife and each holds 40 shares of X's stock—i.e., they have separate ownership of their shares rather than to hold them in cotenancy. As noted in **Ex. (2)**, *A* and *B* are treated as one shareholder, and so the 100–shareholder limitation is satisfied. Two years after *A* and *B* acquired their shares of *X* stock, *A* died and bequeathed his 40 shares of *X* stock to his friend, *R*, who had never been related to *A* or to any other shareholder of *X* by blood or by marriage. Upon *A*'s death, his 40 shares of *X* stock are owned by *A*'s estate. *B* (who was the spouse of *A*) and the estate of *A* are treated as only one shareholder. Therefore, so long as *A*'s estate holds *A*'s 40 shares (and no other shareholders are added), the 100–shareholder limitation will be satisfied. However, when the 40 shares are distributed from the estate to *R*, then *R* and *B* will count as two shareholders, and *X* will then have 101 shareholders.

Once any share of *X* passes from the estate to *R*, *X* will cease to qualify as an S corporation. This can occur prior to any formal distribution of *X* shares to *R*; the shares will be treated as belonging to *R* when the estate of *A* terminates even though the shares had not previously been distributed. Note that if an estate has no reason to continue in operation or has existed for the period reasonably needed to accomplish its goals, the estate will be treated as terminated for income tax purposes even if the estate nominally continues for local law purposes. Treas. Reg. § 1.641(b)–3(a). An estate will not be treated as being unduly prolonged when it has elected under § 6166 to pay the estate tax in installments over a period of years and is kept open until the final installment is made, and where the sole purpose of retaining the S corporation's stock in the estate is to facilitate the payment of the estate tax. Rev. Rul. 76–23. The § 6166 deferral could permit an estate to hold an S corporation's stock for almost 15 years without thereby disqualifying the corporation's election for Subchapter S status.

Ex. (5) The same facts as those stated in **Ex. (1)** except that A is the daughter of B's sister—i.e., A is B's niece. A and B are members of a family within the meaning of § 1361(c)(1) since they are lineal descendants of a common ancestor. A and B are treated as one shareholder, and so the 100–shareholder limitation is not violated. Even if A and B had each held 40 shares of X stock in their individual capacity rather than as co-owners, they would be treated as one shareholder. If there are more than 99 other shareholders, some of whom are members of a different family, each family will count as only one shareholder.

Ex. (6) The Y Corporation has ten shares of voting, common stock outstanding. Y has no other classes of stock outstanding. F holds nine shares of Y's stock, and the remaining one share is held by G. F is an individual who is a citizen of the United States. G is an individual who is a nonresident alien. Since one of its shareholders is a nonresident alien, *Y* does not qualify as an S corporation.

Ex. (7)   The same facts as those stated in **Ex. (6)** except that *G* is a C corporation that is organized under the laws of the State of South Carolina. Since one of *Y*'s shareholders is a person who is not an individual, an estate, or a permissible type of trust, *Y* does not qualify as an S corporation.

Ex. (8)   The same facts as those stated in **Ex. (6)** except that *G* is a partnership. *M* and *N* are the only two partners of *G*, and both *M* and *N* are individuals who are citizens of the United States. For the same reason noted in **Ex. (7)**, *Y* does not qualify as an S corporation.

At one time, an S corporation was prohibited from being affiliated with another corporation, and that meant that it could not own a controlling interest in another corporation. That restriction was deleted from the Code, and so an S corporation can have subsidiaries that are C corporations. However, § 1504(b)(8) prohibits an S corporation from being included in a consolidated return.

§ 2. Qualified Subchapter S Subsidiary (QSub)

With one exception, an S corporation cannot have any of its stock owned by a corporation since corporations are not one of the shareholders permitted by § 1361(b)(1)(B). The one exception to that prohibition is that an S corporation can be a wholly owned subsidiary of another S corporation if the parent S corporation elects to treat the subsidiary as a qualified subchapter S subsidiary (QSub). § 1361(b)(3). If that election is made, the subsidiary S corporation (i.e., the QSub) is not treated as a separate corporate entity. Instead, all of the assets, liabilities, and tax items of the QSub are treated as the assets, liabilities and tax items of the parent S corporation. § 1361(b)(3)(A). In essence, since the corporate identity of the QSub is ignored, the parent S corporation and the QSub are treated as a single corporation for federal tax purposes.

If a corporation that was a QSub ceases to qualify as one (for example, that could occur if the parent S corporation ceases to hold all of the stock of the QSub or if the parent corporation ceases to be an S corporation), the subsidiary is treated as a new corporation that acquired the assets and liabilities of the QSub in exchange for its stock immediately before it ceased to qualify as a QSub. In such a case, the subsidiary corporation is barred for five years from becoming an S corporation or a QSub unless the Commissioner consents. § 1361(b)(3).

An S corporation can own stock of other corporations, and it can have a controlling in-

terest in another corporation regardless of
whether its subsidiary is a C corporation or a
QSub. However, an S corporation cannot file a
consolidated return with another corporation.
§ 1504(b)(8).

§ 3.   Trusts as Shareholders

Prior to 1976, the only permissible shareholders were individuals and estates. Trusts
were not listed as a qualified shareholder. Nevertheless, the question arose as to whether
certain types of trusts might be permitted to
hold stock of an S corporation. While that
question is now resolved by statutory amendments to the Code, the history of the pre-Code
treatment is instructive.

One question that was litigated prior to the
adoption of the Tax Reform Act of 1976 is
whether the use of a voting trust by one or
more shareholders prevents the corporation
from qualifying for Subchapter S treatment. At
the time of the 1976 amendment, a regulation
was in effect that asserted that a voting trust
runs afoul of the prohibition against shareholders' being persons other than an individual or
estate. In A & N Furniture & Appliance Co. v.
United States, 271 F.Supp. 40 (S.D. Ohio
1967), a district court repudiated that regulation. The court argued persuasively that the
purpose of the requirement that only individuals and estates can be shareholders was to

protect the integrity of the limitation on the number of permissible shareholders by preventing corporations and trusts, which may have any number of shareholders or beneficiaries, from holding shares in an S corporation, and that a voting trust does not create that risk since all the beneficiaries already hold shares. The court further held that voting trusts do not violate the one class of stock requirement. The court said that the one class requirement "is directed toward the issuance of two classes of stock and accounting difficulties resulting therefrom, rather than voting powers per se." Id. at 45. The results in subsequent litigation on this issue were mixed. The voting trust issue was resolved by an amendment adopted as part of the Tax Reform Act of 1976 that expressly authorizes the use of voting trusts for stock of an S corporation. § 1361(c)(2)(A)(iv). Each beneficiary of the voting trust is counted as a shareholder of the corporation; and so, for the corporation to qualify as an S corporation, each beneficiary must qualify as a permissible shareholder of an S corporation and each shareholder will count towards the 100 limitation (if they are unrelated).

There also was litigation over whether, despite the specific language of the prior version of the Code, some other types of trust could hold stock in an S corporation. A similar problem to that posed by the voting trust arose where a shareholder transferred stock to a revocable trust or to some other type of so-called "grantor trust" or "Clifford trust." For income tax purposes, the grantor of such a trust is treated as the owner of all or a portion of the trust; and therefore the income, deductions and credits attributable to all or a portion of the trust's assets are allocated directly to the grantor and reported on his income tax return. The "grantor trust" or "Clifford trust" provisions are set forth at §§ 671–677 (Subpart E of Part I of Subchapter J).

If the grantor is treated by the provisions of Subchapter J as the owner of *all* of the interests in a grantor trust, there is good cause to treat the grantor as the actual owner of any shares held by the trustee of that trust for corporate income tax purposes as well. Support for such treatment can be found in other income tax areas. For example, in Rev. Rul. 74–613, the Commissioner ruled that a grantor's transfer of an installment obligation to a revocable trust does not constitute a disposition under [§ 453B] because the grantor is treated as the owner of all of the trust's assets under § 676 (i.e., it was a grantor trust). Nevertheless, in W & W Fertilizer Corp. v. United States, 527 F.2d 621 (Ct. Cls. 1975), the then Court of Claims (now the Federal Circuit) held that the transfer of stock to a revocable trust barred the corporation from qualifying for Subchapter S treatment.

The Tax Reform Act of 1976 amended Subchapter S to permit certain types of trusts to hold stock in an S corporation. The provisions concerning trusts were modified and expanded by amendments in subsequent years. As stated below, the current statute permits Subchapter S stock to be held by a grantor trust if only one person is treated as the owner of all of the trust's assets.

The current provisions concerning trusts, which are set forth in § 1361(c)(2) and (d), authorize seven types of trusts to hold stock in an S corporation. If stock is held by a trust that is not one of the seven authorized types, the corporation cannot qualify for Subchapter S treatment. Also, with one exception, if a trust that had qualified as one of the seven authorized types ceases to qualify, a corporation in which that trust holds stock will cease to qualify for Subchapter S treatment commencing with the date that the trust no longer fits within the authorized list. The one exception, which is set forth in § 1361(d)(4)(A), applies to a "qualified Subchapter S trust" (QSST), which is described later in this section.

In discussing the types of trusts that can hold stock in an S corporation, we omit one type because it has such limited application. Section 1361(c)(2)(A)(vi) permits stock to be held by a trust that constitutes an individual retirement account or Roth IRA, but only as to stock of a bank or depository institution holding company that was held by the trust on October 22, 2004.

Six of the seven types of trusts permitted to hold stock of an S corporation are as follows:

(1) A trust *all* of the assets of which are deemed by §§ 671–678 to be owned by one individual who is a citizen or resident of the United States (i.e., by an individual who qualifies as a shareholder of an S corporation). If the assets of a trust are deemed to be owned by the grantor, the trust is sometimes called a "grantor trust." If under § 678 a trust's assets are deemed to be owned by a third party who is not the grantor (because of powers the third party has over the income or corpus of the trust), the trust is sometimes called a "Mallinckrodt trust." A grantor or a Mallinckrodt trust can hold stock of an S corporation only if *all* of the assets of the trust are treated as owned by only one individual. For purposes of determining whether the corporation qualifies as an S corporation, the individual who is deemed to own the trust's assets rather than the trust itself is treated as the shareholder. § 1361(c)(2)(B)(i).

(2) Upon the death of the deemed owner of the assets of a grantor or Mallinckrodt trust, which trust had qualified to hold

stock of an S corporation under (1) above, the trust will continue to qualify to hold such stock for two years after the death of the deemed owner. § 1361(c)(2)(A)(ii). During this two-year period, the estate of the deceased deemed owner of the trust's assets is treated as the shareholder of the stock of an S corporation that is held by that trust. § 1361(c)(2)(B)(ii). The reason for this extension of the permissible holding period is to give the trustee time to distribute the stock to qualified individuals and thereby prevent a termination of the corporation's Subchapter S status.

(3) If stock of an S corporation that was held by a deceased shareholder is transferred pursuant to the decedent's will from the decedent's estate to a trust (i.e., to a testamentary trust or to a pour-over trust), the trust will be permitted to hold that stock for a two-year period beginning on the day that the stock is transferred to the trust. § 1361(c)(2)(A)(iii). During that two-year period, the holder of the S corporation's stock is deemed to be the estate of the deceased shareholder. § 1361(c)(2)(B)(iii).

As previously noted, the estate of a decedent is permitted to hold stock of an S corporation. Consequently, the S corporation stock of a deceased shareholder who bequeathed that stock to a trust can be held in the decedent's estate while the estate is being administered and, after the stock has been distributed to the trust, can be held by the trust for an additional two years.

(4) A voting trust is permitted to hold the stock of an S corporation. § 1361(c)(2)(A)(iv). Each beneficiary of the voting trust is treated as a shareholder. § 1361(c)(2)(B)(iv). Consequently, each beneficiary is counted in determining whether the corporation does not have more than 100 shareholders; and each beneficiary must be a permissible shareholder of an S corporation for the corporation to qualify as an S corporation.

(5) An "electing small business trust" (ESBT) is permitted to hold stock of an S corporation. § 1361(c)(2)(A)(v). An electing small business trust is defined in § 1361(e). In general, it is a trust none of whose beneficiaries is a person other than an individual, an estate, or certain charitable organizations. To qualify, no interest in the trust can have been obtained by "purchase" (i.e., acquired with a cost basis). A trust is disqualified for characterization as an ESBT if it is either: (1) a trust for which a qualified Subchapter S Trust (QSST) election (de-

scribed below) applies as to any corporation whose stock is held by the trust, (2) a trust that is tax exempt, or (3) a charitable remainder annuity trust or unitrust.

The election to be an ESBT is to be made by the trustee. The election applies to the trust's taxable year for which it was made and for succeeding taxable years unless revoked with the consent of the Commissioner. The election must be made within the same time period that is designated in Treas. Reg. § 1.1361–1(j)(6)(iii) for a QSST election. Treas. Reg. § 1.1361–1(m)(iii). In general, the election must be made within the 16–day and two-month period beginning either on the date on which the trust acquired the S corporation's stock or (if the stock of a C corporation was acquired by the trust before that corporation became an S corporation) on the day on which the corporation's Subchapter S election first became effective.

Where stock of an S corporation is held by an electing small business trust, each potential current beneficiary of the trust is treated as a shareholder for purposes of determining whether the corporation complies with the 100 shareholder limitation. Moreover, each potential current beneficiary must be a person who is permitted to hold stock of an S corporation. A potential current beneficiary for any period is a person who, during that period, is entitled to, or at the discretion of any person may, receive a distribution from the income or principal of the trust. However, the object of an unexercised power of appointment is *not* treated as a potential current beneficiary unless the power is exercised by making an appointment to that person. § 1361(e)(2). The proposed regulations provide an extremely broad definition of what constitutes a power of appointment for purposes of this provision. Prop. Reg. § 1.1361–1(m)(4)(vi).

(6) A special type of trust referred to as a "qualified Subchapter S trust" (QSST) is permitted to hold stock of an S corporation if the income beneficiary of the trust (or his legal representative) makes the election described below. A qualified Subchapter S trust is a trust—

　(A) all of the income (as determined for trust accounting purposes) of which is distributed, or required to be distributed, currently to one individual who is a citizen or resident of the United States, and

(B) the terms of which require that—

(i) during the life of the current income beneficiary, there shall be only one income beneficiary of the trust;

(ii) any corpus distributed during the life of the income beneficiary can be distributed only to that beneficiary;

(iii) the income interest of the current income beneficiary terminates on the earlier of the death of such income beneficiary or the termination of the trust; and

(iv) if the trust terminates during the life of the current income beneficiary, all of the assets of the trust are to be distributed to such beneficiary.

A substantially separate and independent share of a trust is treated as a separate trust. § 1361(d)(3). So, it is not necessary to create a separate trust for each beneficiary; it is sufficient to provide separate terms for each share of a trust of which a different person is the beneficiary. However, unless it is important to have just one trust, it is safer to create separate trusts and not face the question of whether the different interests in a single trust constitute a separate share.

To be a qualified Subchapter S trust, it is not necessary that the trust terminate on the death of an income beneficiary. If, on the death of the current income beneficiary of a qualified Subchapter S trust for which an election has been made, another individual becomes the current income beneficiary of the trust, the trust will continue to qualify to hold the S corporation's stock provided that there is only one current income beneficiary and provided that the other requirements described above are satisfied (including the requirement that the individual who is the current income beneficiary be a citizen or resident of the United States). Once an election for qualification as a Subchapter S trust has been made, it will apply to each qualified successive current income beneficiary, but any such successive beneficiary can rescind an existing election by filing an affirmative refusal to consent within 15 days and 2 months after becoming the income beneficiary. § 1361(d)(2)(B)(ii); Treas. Reg. § 1.1361–1(j)(10).

Except for the provision described above for successive current income beneficiaries, a valid election to be a Subchapter S trust can be revoked only with the consent of the Commissioner. Treas. Reg. § 1.1361–1(j)(11). If a qualified Subchapter S trust ceases to meet any of the requirements of (6)(B) above, from that date forward the trust's holding of stock will disqualify the corporation for Subchapter S treatment; if the trust ceases to meet the requirements of (6)(A) above but continues to meet the requirements of (6)(B), it will not cease to be a qualified Subchapter S trust until the first day of the next taxable year. § 1361(d)(4).

If a valid election is made for a qualified Subchapter S trust, the current income beneficiary is treated for income tax purposes as the owner of the stock of each S corporation that are held by the trust and for which the election was made. If the QSST holds stock in more than one S corporation, the election of the current income beneficiary is made separately with respect to the stock in each S corporation. § 1361(d)(2)(B). If the election is made, the trust will be treated as a Mallinckrodt trust which is permitted to hold stock of that S corporation. § 1361(d)(1). As a consequence, all of the income or losses of the S corporation that would be allocated to the trust will instead be allocated directly to the income beneficiary. However, this pass-through treatment does not apply to the gain or loss recognized by the QSST on a disposition of its S corporation stock. Treas. Reg. § 1.1361–1(j)(8).

Note that when an election is made, the current income beneficiary is treated as the owner of the targeted stock for *income tax purposes* but not for estate tax purposes. Thus, such stock will not be included in the income beneficiary's gross estate on his death unless the terms of the trust are such that the stock is included under normal estate tax rules.

The election for a trust to become a QSST is made by the current income beneficiary. The time, manner and form for a current income beneficiary to make an election are set forth in Treas. Reg. § 1.1361–1(j)(6). In general, with one exception, the election must be made within the 16–day and 2–month period beginning on the date on which the stock is acquired by the trust or on the first day of the corporation's first taxable year for which the Subchapter S election is effective.

There is a grace period of 2 months and 15 days for the election—i.e., it can be made effective for a date up to 2 months and 15 days before the election is filed. § 1361(d)(2)(D). This period corresponds to the two-month and 15–day grace period provided to a corporation and its shareholders to make a valid Subchapter S election.

Ex. *X*, an S corporation, had 90 shares of stock outstanding of which individuals *A*, *B* and *C* each owned 30 shares. In Year One, *A* died and bequeathed his 30 shares of *X* stock in trust under terms described below. After *A*'s death, his 30 shares of *X* stock are held by *A*'s executor for his estate. Since the estate is a permissible shareholder of an S corporation, *X* continues to qualify as an S corporation after *A*'s death.

(a) In August of Year Two, *A*'s executor distributed the stock to the Friendly National Bank as trustee of *A*'s testamentary trust. The trustee did not make an election to have the trust be an electing small business trust (ESBT). The terms of the trust provide that the income is to be distributed currently to *A*'s two adult children for so long as they live, and upon the death of the last to die of those two children, the trust estate is to be distributed *per stirpes* among the issue of *A*'s children. *A*'s children are citizens of the United States. If no such issue survive, the trust corpus is to be distributed to the Salvation Army. During the lifetime of either income beneficiary, the trustee is authorized to invade corpus on behalf of either income beneficiary or both in such amounts and in such proportions as the trustee shall determine in its discretion. The trust does not constitute a qualified Subchapter S trust (QSST) because there is more than one current income beneficiary. The interest of either of the two current income beneficiaries is not sufficiently separate to be treated as a separate trust. The trustee is permitted to hold the stock of X for 2 years without disqualifying X for Subchapter S treatment. If the trustee holds the stock for more than 2 years, X will cease to qualify as an S corporation on the day after that 2–year period expires. However, if prior to that day, the trustee invaded the trust's corpus by distributing its 30 shares of X stock to either income beneficiary or to both, X will continue to qualify as an S corporation. Similarly, the trustee could protect X's election for Subchapter S treatment by selling its 30 shares of X to a person who qualifies as a shareholder of an S corporation if the sale is made within the 2–year period.

(b) If, instead of providing a single testamentary trust, A's will created two trusts, one for each child, and divided the residuary estate equally between those two trusts (so that each trust received 15 shares of X stock), and if each trust contained the same provisions as the single trust described above, except that each trust would have only one income beneficiary and the trustee could invade corpus only on behalf of that beneficiary, then each of the two trusts would constitute a qualified Subchapter S trust. No election was made to make either of the trusts an electing small business trust (ESBT). If each of the two income beneficiaries made a timely election to be treated as the owner for income tax purposes of the 15 shares of X stock that is held in that beneficiary's trust, the two trusts can continue to hold the X stock after the 2–year period has expired without disqualifying X for Subchapter S treatment. If one of the beneficiaries makes such an election and the other does not, then X will cease to qualify as an S corporation on the day after the 2–year period for the trust for the nonelecting beneficiary expires unless the trust for the nonelecting beneficiary disposes of its 15 shares of X stock (e.g., by distributing those shares to its beneficiary) within 2 years after acquiring those shares.

(c) The same result as that reached in (b) above can be obtained by using a single testamentary trust in which the interest of each current income beneficiary is stated in separate and independent terms so that the two separate shares will be treated as separate trusts for purposes of Subchapter S.

§ 4. Nominal Stock Ownership

Even prior to the statutory liberalization of the restrictions prohibiting a trustee's ownership of stock of an S corporation, those restrictions were deemed not to apply to a person who held stock as a mere nominee, agent, guardian or custodian of an individual; the person on whose behalf such stock is held is treated as the shareholder. Treas. Reg. § 1.1361–1(e)(1). Thus, where stock is held by a custodian for a minor under either the Uniform Gift to Minors Act or the Uniform Transfers to Minors Act, the minor (and not the custodian) is deemed to be the shareholder. Treas. Reg. § 1.1361–1(e)(1). Therefore, the custodian can be a person who is not qualified to own stock of an S corporation, such as a partnership or a nonresident alien. The consent of a minor must be made by the minor or by the legal representative of the minor (or, if none, by a natural or adopted parent of the minor). Treas. Reg. § 1.1362–6(b)(2)(ii).

§ 5. One Class of Stock Requirement

An S corporation is not permitted to have more than one class of stock. § 1361(b)(1)(D). In the past, the question of whether a corporation has two classes of stock (in contravention of that requirement) arose in a number of routine circumstances that frequently arise in the relationship between a corporation and its shareholders—for example, where a shareholder had given another a proxy to vote his stock and where a purported debt instrument was characterized as an equity investment (hybrid stock). Those issues have been resolved.

A prior regulation, which has been deleted, prohibited the existence of different voting rights in the corporation's stock. Relying on that regulation, the Commissioner ruled in Rev. Rul. 63–226 that the granting of an irrevocable proxy violated the one class of stock requirement. However, in Parker Oil Co. v. Commissioner, 58 T.C. 985 (1972), acq. in result, a majority of the Tax Court held that the existence of an irrevocable proxy to vote shares of the corporation's stock did not create a second class of stock and did not disqualify a Subchapter S election. The court held that the then existing regulation was invalid insofar as it required that all shares of stock must have identical voting rights, and the court held that Rev. Rul. 63–226 is incorrect. The Commissioner then revoked Rev. Rul. 63–226 and promulgated Rev. Rul. 73–611, in which, while apparently conceding that an irrevocable proxy does not create a second class of stock, the Commissioner stated that if disproportionate voting rights were created by the corporate charter, as contrasted to shareholder agreements, the differences in voting rights would violate the one class of stock requirement.

This issue was laid to rest by the SRA (the Subchapter S Revision Act of 1982) which added § 1361(c)(4) to the Code. Section 1361(c)(4) provides that differences in voting rights of common stock are disregarded in determining whether a corporation has more than one class of stock. Since an S corporation can have only one class of stock, the question of the consequence of there being a proxy to vote the stock can arise only in connection with common stock; and so the limitation of the statute to common stock has no significance. Moreover, Treas. Reg. § 1.1361–1(*l*)(1) now expressly authorizes proxy agreements.

The question of whether a corporation has two classes of stock was also raised in connection with the transfer of stock to a voting trust. In light of § 1361(c)(2)(A)(iv) (permitting the use of a voting trust), that is no longer an issue—that is, the Commissioner could not successfully contend that the existence of a voting trust for some shares of stock but not for others creates two classes of stock. Moreover, as noted above, the SRA's addition to the Code of § 1361(c)(4), which provides that differences in voting rights of common stock are disregarded in determining whether there is more than one class of stock, is dispositive. In 1992, Treasury adopted final regulations that make the one class of stock requirement turn exclusively on whether the "outstanding shares of stock of the corporation confer identical rights to distri-

bution and liquidation proceeds." Treas. Reg.
§ 1.1361–1(*l*)(1). As to differences in voting
rights, that regulation states:

> Differences in voting rights among shares of
> stock of a corporation are disregarded in
> determining whether a corporation has more
> than one class of stock. Thus, if all shares of
> stock of an S corporation have identical
> rights to distribution and liquidation pro-
> ceeds, the corporation may have voting and
> nonvoting common stock, a class of stock
> that may vote only on certain issues, irrevo-
> cable proxy agreements, or groups of shares
> that differ with respect to rights to elect
> members of the board of directors.

The effect on the question of whether it has
more than one class of stock when a corporation makes disproportionate distributions on
its shares of stock or makes distributions to
some shareholders earlier than to others is
examined in Section 5(g) of this chapter.

(a) Hybrid Stock

Corporate debt may be treated as stock for
many tax purposes when a debt instrument
bears too many of the characteristics of equity
investment. For convenience, purported debt
instruments that are treated as stock for tax
purposes are sometimes referred to herein as
"hybrid stock." If a corporation had hybrid
stock outstanding, there previously was a regulation that provided that the hybrid stock "will

generally constitute a second class of stock" for Subchapter S purposes unless the hybrid stock is owned by the nominal stockholders in substantially the same proportion as they own their nominal stock. The Service suffered one failure after another in litigating the validity of that statement. Two courts of appeals and the Tax Court held that that statement was invalid and that hybrid stock generally will not constitute a second class of stock. The Service enjoyed a fleeting success when a panel of the Seventh Circuit sustained the validity of that prior regulation in a divided decision in Portage Plastics Co. v. United States, 470 F.2d 308 (7th Cir. 1972), but upon a rehearing en banc, the Seventh Circuit vacated the panel's decision and held that the regulation was invalid and that hybrid stock usually will not constitute a second class of stock. 486 F.2d 632 (7th Cir. 1973) (en banc).

The courts rejected the previous language of the regulations on hybrid stock because they concluded that Congress did not intend to discourage debt financing for Subchapter S corporations and that a threat of a retroactive disqualification would do so. The courts believed that the regulation would frustrate the legislative purpose of Subchapter S to minimize tax considerations as a factor in determining the form in which a business will be conducted. In essence, the courts held that while a debt may be treated as stock for some tax purposes (such as the denial of an interest deduction and the treatment of "loan" amortization payments as dividends), it does not constitute stock for the purposes of Subchapter S.

The courts did not hold that hybrid stock could never be treated as a second class of stock, but rather they rejected a blanket coverage of all disproportionately held hybrid stock and suggested that it is only in rare circumstances that a debt will constitute a second class of stock. For example, in the 1973 en banc decision of *Portage Plastics*, the Seventh Circuit stated that if a corporation gave notes to its investors instead of giving them its stock in order to accomplish some tax avoidance purpose (such as to satisfy the one class of stock requirement or to avoid the limitation on the number of shareholders) and if the parties' characterization of the "loans" as a debt were a sham, the notes could be treated as a second class of stock. We will see that the regulation that was adopted in 1992 (and amended in 1995), adopts a similar approach to that taken by the court in *Portage Plastics*.

If hybrid stock is not treated as a second class of stock, the question arises as to the manner in which the S corporation's tax attributes are to be allocated among its shareholders when there is hybrid stock. Presumably, no allocation will be made to the hybrid stock since the basis of the *Portage Plastics* decision, and of the current regulation adopting that approach, is that such debt is not treated as "stock" for purposes of Subchapter S.

The current regulations expressly state that "straight debt," a classification of a specific type of debt (described below) that the Code prohibits from being treated as a second class of stock, will *generally* be treated as debt for other tax purposes even when it would have been treated as an equity interest under general tax law principles if the straight debt safe harbor were not applicable. Treas. Reg. § 1.1361–1(*l*)(5)(iv). Accordingly, interest paid on such debt *generally* will be treated as interest rather than as a distribution to a shareholder. There is no reason that the same treatment should not apply to other forms of what otherwise would be hybrid stock of an S corporation—i.e. they will be treated as true debt. However, the regulation cryptically states that if the interest payable on straight debt is unreasonably high, an appropriate portion of the interest "may be recharacterized and treated" as something else. The regulation does not say what the recharacterization might be, but it does state that it will not cause a second class of stock treatment.

(1) *Straight Debt*

As to the characterization of debt as a second class of stock, the SRA added § 1361(c)(5) to the Code, which provides a safe harbor for so-called "straight debt." Straight debt is not treated as a second class of stock. Indeed, for tax purposes, straight debt generally is treated as a genuine debt of the corporation, rather than as stock, and is subject to the rules of the tax law that apply to indebtedness Treas. Reg. § 1.1361–1(l)(5)(iv). Straight debt is defined in § 1361(c)(5)(B) as a written unconditional promise to pay a sum certain in money on a specified date or on demand if:

(1) the interest rate and payment dates are not contingent on profits, the borrower's discretion, the payment of dividends with respect to common stock, or similar factors,

(2) the debt is not convertible (directly or indirectly) into stock or other equity interests of the corporation, and

(3) the creditor is an individual (other than a nonresident alien), an estate, a trust that qualifies as a permissible shareholder of stock of an S corporation, or a person that is actively and regularly engaged in the business of lending money.

The fact that a debt is subordinated to other obligations of the corporation does not prevent it from qualifying as straight debt. Treas. Reg. § 1.1361–1(l)(5)(ii).

The exemption of straight debt from second class of stock treatment is described in the Code and in the regulation as a safe harbor. That description would seem to negate an in-

ference, which the statute otherwise might
have created, that debt that does not qualify as
straight debt, and that under ordinary tax
principles would be characterized as hybrid
stock, will constitute a second class of stock.

You will recall that *Portage Plastics* does not
insulate all types of hybrid stock from second
class characterization. In its en banc decision,
the Seventh Circuit stated that hybrid stock
that was created for the purpose of evading
some statutory requirement (such as the maximum shareholder limitation or the second class
of stock requirement) can constitute a second
class of stock. The straight debt provision likely was intended as a safe harbor in which
taxpayers who comply are insulated from the
risk that a debt instrument would constitute a
second class of stock under the *Portage Plastics*
definition.

Professor Martin D. Ginsburg, who played a
significant role in the drafting and adoption of
the 1982 SRA (which Act included the adoption
of the straight debt provision), confirms that
Treasury and Congress did not intend by the
1982 SRA to overrule *Portage Plastics*. Instead,
according to Ginsburg, Congress intended to
leave the hybrid stock treatment of *Portage
Plastics* intact, subject to the straight debt safe
harbor.

Contrary to the foregoing, in the preamble to
the 1990 set of proposed regulations on second

class of stock that the Treasury promulgated on October 5, 1990, Treasury stated that the legislative history of the 1982 SRA indicates that Congress intended that the straight debt provision supplant the *Portage Plastics* decision. Accordingly, the preamble stated, "consistent with congressional intent, this pre–1982 case law is not reflected in these proposed regulations, and a purported debt instrument that is outside the safe harbor rules will be treated as a second class of stock for Subchapter S purposes if it constitutes equity under general principles of Federal tax law." The legislative history to which the preamble referred consists of the statement in both the Senate and House Reports on the 1982 SRA that, "The classification of an instrument outside the safe harbor rules as stock or debt will be made under usual tax law classification principles." However, the October, 1982 report of the Joint Committee staff on the 1982 SRA clarified that sentence by restating it to read, "The classification of instruments outside the safe harbor rule as stock or debt will be made under usual tax law classification principles *applicable to subchapter S corporations.*" [Emphasis added.]

The 1990 proposed regulations were revised and subsequently replaced by final regulations that were adopted in 1992. The final regulations adopted the approach taken in *Portage Plastics*.

An obligation that qualified as straight debt will cease to qualify if either it is modified so that its terms no longer comply with the definition of straight debt, or it is transferred to a person who does not qualify as a permissible shareholder of an S corporation. Treas. Reg. § 1.1361–1(*l*)(5)(iii).

(2) Current Treatment of Debt Instruments

The current regulations (Treas. Reg. § 1.-1361–1(*l*)(4)) set forth a general rule concerning debt instruments that emulates the *Portage Plastics* approach and also establishes a number of safe harbors (including the straight debt safe harbor) that immunize certain debt instruments from second class of stock treatment regardless of the applicability of the general rule. This regulatory provision applies to an instrument, obligation or arrangement (other than stock) that provides some rights against the corporation (whether or not designated as a debt instrument). For convenience, hereafter we will sometimes refer to all such instruments, obligations and arrangements as "debt instruments."

A debt instrument will not be treated as a second class of stock unless *both* of the following two conditions exist: (1) the debt instrument is treated by the general principles of federal tax law as an equity interest in the corporation or causes the holder thereof to be treated by federal tax law as a shareholder; and

(2) a principal purpose of issuing the debt instrument (or entering into the arrangement) is to circumvent either the requirement that all outstanding stock of an S corporation have identical rights to distribution and liquidation proceeds or the requirement that the number of shareholders cannot exceed a specified figure. Treas. Reg. § 1.1361–1(*l*)(4)(ii)(A). Because of this second requirement, a debt instrument will not constitute a second class of stock unless the subjective principal purpose of evading a statutory requirement is found to exist. It seems unlikely that there will be many cases in which that principal purpose exists (much less can be proved), and so most debt instruments will not cause a loss of S corporation status.

In addition to establishing a narrow general rule for treating a debt instrument as a second class of stock, the regulations provide a number of safe harbors that preclude second class of stock treatment regardless of the debt instrument's characterization under that general rule. Some of those safe harbors are:

    (1) *Proportionately-held obligations.* Debt instruments (and obligations) of the same class that are held only by shareholders and are held proportionately to their stock holdings are not treated as a second class of stock. For example, if all of such debt instruments are held by a sole shareholder, they are held proportionate-

ly to the stock holdings and cannot constitute a second class of stock.

(2) *Short-term unwritten advances.* A shareholder's unwritten advances to the corporation that are treated as debt by the parties and are expected to be repaid within a reasonable time are not treated as a second class of stock. This provision applies only if the aggregate of such unwritten advances by that shareholder do not exceed $10,000 at any time during the corporation's taxable year.

(3) *Deferred compensation.* A debt instrument issued to an employee or independent contractor representing deferred compensation for services rendered is not treated as stock if certain conditions described in Treas. Reg. § 1.1361–1(b)(4) are satisfied.

(4) *Straight debt.* As noted in Section 5(a)(1) of this chapter, § 1361(c)(5) provides a safe harbor for so-called "straight debt," and the provision is included in the regulations with some elaboration. Treas. Reg. § 1.1361–1(*l*)(5).

(3) Comments on the Regulatory Treatment of Debt

In the view of the authors, the treatment of debt that was adopted in the current regulations makes far more sense than the position that Treasury initially adopted in the 1990 proposed regulations. Treasury properly discarded its earlier position on this issue. The policies at stake in deciding whether an S corporation's obligation should be treated as debt or equity are significantly different from those at stake in deciding how a C corporation's obligation should be treated. In the typical C corporation context, the "integrity" of the double-tax system is at issue since dividends create income for a shareholder without generating a deduction for the corporation. In the typical S corporation context, however, dividends have nothing to do with double taxation. All that should be at issue is whether the corporation's capital structure has become so complex that it either is not feasible or for some reason is inappropriate to characterize the entity as a "small business corporation"—a question that has no logical connection with whether a similar C corporation is escaping the double tax.

(b) Call Options

A call option, warrant or similar instrument that is issued by a corporation is included within the instruments or arrangements that can be classified as a second class of stock. For convenience, all of these types of instruments and arrangements are referred to collectively as "call options." The regulations have several provisions, including safe harbors, that address call options.

The general principle is that a call option will not be treated as a second class of stock unless, after taking into account all the facts and circumstances: (1) the call option is substantially certain to be exercised (either by the holder or by a potential transferee), and (2) the call option has a strike price (i.e., the price payable for the stock on exercise of the option) that is substantially below the fair market value of the underlying stock. In determining whether the strike price is substantially below the fair market value of the underlying stock, the value of the underlying stock is determined at the date on which the call option was issued. A strike price will not violate the requirement that it is not substantially less then the stock's fair market value if the terms of the call option are such that the strike price cannot be less than the fair market value of the underlying stock at the time of exercise. Treas. Reg. § 1.1361–1(l)(4)(iii)(A).

However, if a call option subsequently is either materially modified or transferred from a person who is eligible to be a shareholder of an S corporation to a person who is ineligible, then the call option must be retested on that date. Treas. Reg. § 1.1361–1(l)(4)(v), Ex. (1). The call option will cease to qualify under the general rule if, at that subsequent date, the option fails both of the tests noted above. While that regulation does not specify the extent to which a strike price must be below the stock's fair market value to be substantial, the example treats a strike price that is 50% of the stock's value as substantially below that value.

If a call option is issued in connection with a loan to the corporation, an extension of the exercise period of the option will not constitute a "material modification" if the extension is made in connection with and consistent with a modification of the terms of the loan. Treas. Reg. § 1.1361–1(l)(4)(iii)(A).

In addition to the general principle for determining whether a call option constitutes a second class of stock, the regulations provide several safe harbors.

(1) A call option will not be a second class of stock if at the date that the option is issued, materially modified, or transferred by an eligible person to an ineligible person, the strike price of the option is at least equal to 90% of the fair market value of the underlying stock at that date. A good faith determination of fair market value by the corporation will be respected unless the determination was substantially in error and was not made with reasonable diligence. Treas. Reg. § 1.1361–1(l)(4)(iii)(C).

(2) A call option does not constitute a second class of stock if it is issued to a person who is actively and regularly engaged in the business of lending and is issued in

connection with a commercially reasonable loan to the corporation. This safe harbor continues to apply if the call option is transferred in connection with a transfer of the loan, but it terminates if the call option is otherwise transferred. Treas. Reg. § 1.1361–1(*l*)(4)(iii)(B).

(3) A call option that is issued to an employee or independent contractor who performed services for the corporation or for a related corporation (and that is not excessive compensation) is not treated as a second class of stock if the call option is nontransferable (as defined in Treas. Reg. § 1.83–3(d)) and does not have a readily ascertainable fair market value at the time that it is issued. Treas. Reg. § 1.1361–1(*l*)(4)(iii)(B). This safe harbor conforms the S corporation regulations with the treatment of such options under § 83 of the Code—i.e., for general income tax purposes, the receipt of such an option typically will not be included in the recipient's income until it is transferred or exercised. See Treas. Reg. § 1.83–7. If the call option subsequently becomes transferable, this safe harbor will cease to apply.

(4) The regulations authorize the Commissioner to promulgate additional exceptions and safe harbors by Revenue Rul-

ings or other publications. Treas. Reg.
§ 1.1361–1(*l*)(4)(iii)(B)(3).

(c) Convertible Debt

Convertible debt is treated for this purpose
as if it is both a debt instrument and a call
option, and it will be tested under the standards used for both of those instruments. If it
fails either test, it will be a second class of
stock. Thus, a convertible debt will constitute a
second class of stock if it would be so treated
under *either* the principles described above that
pertain to debt instruments or those that pertain to call options. Treas. Reg. § 1.1361–
1(*l*)(4)(iv).

(d) Restricted Stock

With only a few exceptions, all of the outstanding stock of a corporation is taken into
account in determining whether the corporation's equity provides identical distribution and
liquidation rights so that there is only one class
of stock. One of the exceptions is for restricted
stock (i.e., stock that is "substantially nonvested") that is issued for services performed.

Under § 83, when a person receives stock for
services performed and when the stock is "substantially nonvested," the stock is not included
in the income of the recipient and the recipient
is not treated as the owner of such restricted
stock until it becomes substantially vested.
Treas. Reg. § 1.83–1(a)(1). For this purpose,

stock is "substantially nonvested" if it is non-transferable and is subject to a substantial risk of forfeiture. Treas. Reg. § 1.83–3(b). However, § 83(b) permits the recipient of restricted stock to elect to recognize income on its receipt (notwithstanding that it is substantially nonvested), and the recipient is treated as the owner of restricted stock for which that election has been made. Treas. Reg. § 1.83–2(a).

The current regulations for S corporations track the treatment of restricted stock that is established for general income tax purposes by § 83. When restricted stock (i.e., stock that is substantially nonvested) is issued in connection with the performance of services, it is treated as not being outstanding stock of the corporation for so long as it remains substantially nonvested, and so it has no effect on the determination of whether the corporation has a second class of stock outstanding. However, if the recipient of the restricted stock makes an election under § 83(b) to have the stock included in the recipient's income, it will be treated as outstanding stock and will constitute a second class of stock unless it provides identical rights to distributions and liquidation that the other outstanding shares of the corporation's stock possess. Treas. Reg. § 1.1361–1(b)(3).

(e) Buy–Sell Arrangements

Buy-sell agreements among shareholders (so-called cross-purchase buy-sell arrangements), redemption agreements, and agreements restricting the transferability of stock will not cause second class of stock treatment unless the principal purpose of the arrangement is to circumvent the one class of stock requirement *and* the agreement establishes a purchase price that is substantially above or below the fair market value of the stock at the time at which the agreement was made. Treas. Reg. § 1.1361–1(*l*)(2)(iii). All three types of these arrangements are hereinafter referred to collectively as "buy-sell agreements."

A buy-sell agreement that provides for the purchase or redemption of stock at book value or at a price that lies between book value and the fair market value of the stock will not be treated as establishing a price that is substantially above or below the fair market value of the stock. Id. Thus, a safe harbor is provided when the price is set anywhere between book value and fair market value, inclusive.

A good faith determination of fair market value will be respected unless it can be shown that the valuation was substantially in error and that the determination of value was not made with reasonable diligence. A determination of book value will be respected if either: (1) the book value is determined in accordance with Generally Accepted Accounting Principles, or (2) the determination of book value is used for any substantial nontax purpose. Id.

In addition, the regulations create a safe harbor under which a bona fide agreement to redeem or purchase stock at the time of death, divorce, disability, or termination of employment will not cause second class of stock classification. Id. The meaning of the "bona fide" requirement is not stated, but it is clear that it does not require an accurate or near-accurate price. See Treas. Reg. § 1.1361–1(*l*)(2)(vi), Ex. (9). It seems likely that the reference to "bona fide" requires only that the arrangement be at arm's length, and that it can apply to agreements among related parties. Given the special goals that attend a buy-sell agreement among shareholders of a corporation, it is not easy to determine what standard should be employed to determine whether an arrangement was bona fide. That is, the price set for a buy-out between a shareholder and a person who holds no current interest in the corporation may be quite different from the price set by a mutual buy-out arrangement among shareholders. In the latter case, the shareholders do not know which of them will be the survivor, and so they will likely give weight to considerations concerning how much can be paid for a deceased or retiring shareholder's stock without impairing the ability of the corporation to continue in business. This is a legitimate arm's length business consideration and should be considered bona fide, but the definition of the bona fide standard is unsettled.

(f) Illustrations

Ex. (1)   *A* and *B* are equal shareholders of *X*, an S corporation. *A* makes a substantial loan to the corporation, and the resulting "debt" to *A* is treated as an equity interest (i.e., as hybrid stock) for general federal tax purposes. The corporation's obligation to pay annual interest is contingent on its having a specified minimum amount of profits, and so the "debt" does not qualify as straight debt. Unless a principal purpose of making the "loan" was to circumvent the one class of stock requirement (obviously, there was no reason to seek evasion of the limitation on the number of permissible shareholders), the debt will not be treated as a second class of stock. If the debt does not constitute a second class of stock (because the prohibited principal purpose did not exist), it is likely that the "interest" payments made by *X* on the purported debt instrument will be treated as interest for general federal tax purposes rather than as distributions from the corporation. See Treas. Reg. § 1.1361–1(*l*)(5)(iv).

Ex. (2)   The same facts as those stated in **Ex. (1)** except that the "loan" to *X* was made equally by *A* and *B*. Since the "debt" is held proportionately by the shareholders of *X*, it comes within a safe harbor. There is no need for the taxpayers to prove that the transaction lacked a purpose of evading the one class of stock requirement (albeit, that would be an easy task). The safe harbor mandates that the purported debt is not treated as a second class of stock.

Ex. (3)   *A*, *B* and *C* are equal shareholders of *X*, an S corporation. The shareholders and *X* enter into an agreement under which the stock of a shareholder is to be redeemed by the corporation upon the death or divorce of that shareholder. Such arrangements are sometimes referred to as an "entity buy-out agreement" or as a "redemption agreement." The price to be paid for the redemption of a deceased or divorced shareholder's stock is substantially less than the fair market value and the book value of that stock. There is a bona fide business purpose to the agreement. Because the redemption agreement is triggered only by the divorce or death of a shareholder, it falls within a safe harbor, and the agreement does not cause second class of stock treatment.

Ex. (4)   The same facts as those stated in **Ex. (3)** except that the redemption agreement also provides for the redemption of *A*'s stock in the event that *X*'s profits for a subsequent year fall below a stated figure. The price to be paid for the redemption of *A*'s stock is substantially less than the fair market value and the book value of that stock. The redemption agreement will not cause second class of stock characterization unless a principal purpose of the provision concerning the redemption of *A*'s stock was to circumvent the one class of stock requirement. The agreement concerning *A*'s stock is not protected by a safe harbor provision, and so it must satisfy the general principle concerning buy-sell agreements to escape second class of stock treatment.

Ex. (5) The same facts as those stated in **Ex. (4)** except that, while the price to be paid for the redemption of *A*'s stock is substantially less than the stock's fair market value, the price is equal to the book value of that stock. The book value of the stock is determined under Generally Accepted Accounting Principles. The regulations state that if an agreement provides that stock is to be redeemed or purchased at book value or at a price between book and fair market value, it will not be treated as establishing a price that is substantially below or above fair market value. This provision applies only if book value is determined in accordance with Generally Accepted Accounting Principles or is used for any substantial nontax purpose. Since that provision applies to the instant facts, the redemption agreement will not cause second class of stock treatment.

(g) Differences in Amounts or Timing of Actual Distributions

The 1990 proposed regulations went much further than merely disqualifying from Subchapter S treatment corporations that have hybrid stock outstanding. While confirming that the crucial question in determining whether stock is to be treated as part of a single class is whether they confer *identical* rights to distribution and liquidation proceeds, the 1990 proposed regulations adopted a very strict construction of the requirement that such rights be identical. Unless one of several limited exceptions applied, the 1990 proposed regulations treated a corporation as having more than one class of stock whenever there was unequal timing or amount of distributions on stock shares regardless of whether the difference was established as a *right* by the articles, charter, bylaws, state law, administrative action or by agreement, or whether a variance in the amount or timing of distributions occurred inadvertently. The existence of virtually any variance in rights or in actual distributions would cause there to be more than one class of stock and so disqualify an S election.

The 1990 proposed regulations were subjected to severe criticism. One major object of that criticism was the treatment of differences in amounts or timing of distributions that were not established in a "governing provision." The 1990 proposed regulations treated virtually all of such differences, even though not created by a governing provision, as creating more than one class of stock. In response to the comments it had received, Treasury revised and supplanted the 1990 proposed regulations so as to eliminate that offending treatment (as well as several others). The current regulations, which were adopted in 1992, restrict the determination of identity of stock rights to the *rights* that governing provisions provide to the stockholders to receive current and liquidating distributions from the corporation. The following is a summary of most of the terms of the current final regulations.

A corporation is treated as having only one class of stock if all outstanding shares of the corporation's stock confer identical rights to distribution and liquidation proceeds. With only a few exceptions, the identity of rights requirement applies to the timing of distributions as well as to the amounts distributed. Differences in voting rights are ignored. The determination of whether shares of stock possess identical rights rests exclusively on the terms of "governing provisions." The governing provisions consist of the: "corporate charter, articles of incorporation, bylaws, applicable state law, and binding agreements relating to distribution and liquidation proceeds." Treas. Reg. § 1.1361–1(l)(2)(i). That is an exclusive list, and only rights created by a governing provision are taken into account for this purpose.

A commercial contractual agreement such as a lease, employment agreement, or loan agreement does not constitute "a binding agreement relating to distribution and liquidation proceeds" unless a principal purpose of that agreement was to circumvent the one class of stock requirement. Id. Thus, unless the facts and circumstances demonstrate that the prohibited principal purpose exists, such commercial contractual agreements will not constitute a governing provision and therefore will not cause there to be more than one class of stock.

While differences in timing or amounts of distributions (including actual, constructive and deemed distributions) that do not occur because of a governing provision do not cause a second class of stock treatment, the regulations warn that such differences can cause other income tax consequences. Treas. Reg. § 1.1361–1(l)(2)(vi), Exs. (3), (4). The regulations offer little guidance as to the nature of those potential tax consequences, other than to suggest that a difference in timing might cause recharacterization of part of the distributions under § 7872 (dealing with certain loans bearing inadequate interest) or some other provision.

There is reason to question the seriousness of this threat. It does not seem likely that the Service would seek a recharacterization unless there was a substantial amount involved. Even then, it would not be a simple matter to establish a recharacterization when the difference is solely one of timing. For example, if there is a difference in the timing of distributions, would the corporation be deemed to have made a "loan" to the recipients of the earlier distribution so that a distribution to the shareholder and a return of an interest payment could be imputed under § 7872?

When there is a difference as to the amounts of distributions, it might be easier to find that there was a gift or compensation from one shareholder to another, but even that might be difficult to establish in many circumstances.

Consequently, when, pursuant to an employment agreement, an S corporation pays excessive compensation to an employee who is also a shareholder, or when excessive fringe benefits are paid to a shareholder-employee, those payments will not violate the one class of stock requirement if the agreement to make those payments was not made principally in order to circumvent the one class of stock requirement. If an S corporation makes a loan to a shareholder at a below-market interest rate, there can be a constructive distribution to the shareholder under § 7872. The constructive distribution will not create a second class of stock unless the parties entered into the loan agreement principally in order to circumvent the one class of stock requirement. Treas. Reg. § 1.1361–1(*l*)(2)(vi), Ex. (5). Such agreements do not constitute governing provisions unless they were made for the prohibited principal purpose.

The list of governing provisions includes "applicable state law." Thus, when state law creates different distribution or liquidation rights among shareholders, that will create more than one class of stock. An example of this is set forth in Treas. Reg. § 1.1361–1(*l*)(2)(vi), Ex. (1). In that example, state law required that persons who obtained stock from a corporation in exchange for property in kind must waive all rights to distributions until the shareholders who obtained stock for cash contributions receive distributions equal to their cash contributions. Since state law created unequal rights to distributions among the shareholders, the corporation had more than one class of stock outstanding and cannot qualify as an S corporation.

The following examples illustrate the operation of the identical rights requirement.

Ex. (1)   *A* and *B* are equal shareholders of *X*, an S corporation, and are entitled to equal distributions from the corporation. *X* distributes $50,000 to *A* in November, Year One, and distributes $50,000 to *B* in October, Year Two. The difference in the timing of these two distributions was not established by a governing provision. The difference in timing will not cause a second class of stock characterization and so will not terminate an S election. However, the timing disparity may trigger other tax consequences such as the constructive receipts and payments imposed by § 7872 on low or no interest rate loans.

Ex. (2)   *A* and *B* own all of the outstanding stock
of *Y*, an S corporation. The shareholders
are employed by *Y* under a binding employment agreement which sets the compensation for each employee. The
amount of compensation paid to *A* is
reasonable, but the amount of compensation paid to *B* is excessive. Under Treas.
Reg. § 1.162–7, the amount of *B*'s compensation that is excessive is not deductible by *Y* and may constitute a dividend-
type distribution from the corporation.
The facts and circumstances do not indi-
cate that a principal purpose of the com-
pensatory agreement was to circumvent
the one class of stock requirement. Since
the employment agreement is not a governing provision, it does not cause second class of stock treatment. The regulations do not address the question of how
the excess payment to *B* should be treated. It seems likely that the excess payment will be treated as a corporate distribution, which is subject to § 1368. If
so, the excess payment could cause dividend treatment to *B* (if *Y* has accumulated earnings and profits and has no or an
insufficient accumulated adjustments account) or it could reduce *B*'s basis in his
stock.

Ex. (3)   The same facts as those stated in **Ex. (2)**
except that the facts and circumstances
demonstrate that a principal purpose of
providing excessive compensation to *B* in
the employment agreement was to circumvent the one class of stock requirement. In that event, the employment

agreement constitutes a governing provision. Since the excess compensation to *B* constitutes a corporate distribution to him, *Y*'s outstanding shares of stock do not provide identical rights to distribution, and *Y* therefore has more than one class of stock outstanding. *Y* does not qualify for Subchapter S treatment.

Ex. (4) *C* and *D* each owns 50% of the outstanding stock of *Z*, an S corporation. *Z* makes a below-market loan to *C* to which § 7872 applies. Under § 7872, *Z* is deemed to have made a distribution to *C* on account of *C*'s stock holdings in *Z*. If the facts and circumstances do not demonstrate that a principal purpose of the below-market loan was to circumvent the one class of stock requirement, the imputed distribution to *C* will not cause there to be a second class of stock. In such case, it is likely that the constructive distribution to *C* will constitute a distribution under § 1368 and so can cause dividend or basis reduction consequences. On the other hand, if the facts and circumstances demonstrate that circumvention of the one class of stock requirement was a principal purpose of the loan, then the loan agreement becomes a governing provision, and *Z* will be deemed to have a second class of stock.

§ 6.   Election

The provisions of Subchapter S apply only to corporations that have made a valid election to be an S corporation. An election is made by the corporation's filing Form 2553 together with consents signed by each person who is a shareholder on the date that the election is made. § 1362(a); Treas. Reg. § 1.1362–1(a), 6(a)(2). A shareholder's consent must be in the form of a written statement, containing the information required by Treas. Reg. § 1.1362–6(b)(1), and signed by the shareholder under penalties of perjury. A shareholder's consent can be made either in a separate written statement or on Form 2553. While the shareholders' consents should be filed at the same time as the corporation's election, in certain circumstances described in Treas. Reg. § 1.1362–6(b)(3)(iii) a shareholder's consent can be made later. Once a valid election has been made, there is no requirement that persons who subsequently become shareholders consent even when they become shareholders before the election takes effect. Treas. Reg. § 1.1362–6(b)(3)(ii), Ex. (2).

Note that if an S corporation's election is terminated, then, subject to a waiver by the Service, the corporation (or successor corporation) is barred for a period of five years from the date of that termination from making a new election to be an S corporation. § 1362(g). See Section 5 of Chapter 7, infra. However, in certain circumstances where the termination was inadvertent, the corporation may obtain relief from that disqualification by making a request of the Commissioner under § 1362(f).

A valid election can be made at any time in the taxable year preceding the year in which the election first becomes effective. Also, a valid election that is made before the 16th day of the third month after the first day of a taxable year can make that corporation an S corporation as of the beginning of that same taxable year provided that: (1) the corporation met all of the requirements of a "small business corporation" (as defined in § 1361(b)) for each day of that taxable year up to the day of the election; and (2) every person who held stock in the corporation during that taxable year prior to the election makes a timely consent to the election. § 1362(b). If the corporation fails either of those two requirements or if the election is made after the 15th day of the third month, the election will not be effective for that taxable year but will be effective for the first day of the following taxable year. Id. However, if the only reason that the election was not effective for the beginning of the taxable year when made is that the election was not made timely, a late election will be permitted if the Commissioner determines that there was reasonable cause for the failure to make a timely election. § 1362(b)(3), (5). In the latter event, the Commissioner can treat the election as having been timely made for that year.

Ex.   On January 1 of Year One, *A*, *B* and *C* were equal shareholders of the *X* Corporation which reports its income on a calendar year basis. *A* died on January 20 of Year One and bequeathed his estate to his brother, *M*. *A* named a bank as his executor. On March 10 of Year One, *X* filed its election to be an S corporation together with consents executed by *B*, *C*, and the executor of *A*'s estate. (*A*'s shares of *X* were still held by his executor on behalf of *A*'s estate.) *X* qualified as a small business corporation on every day of Year One. The election made by *X* is valid, but does it apply retroactively to January 1 of Year One? To apply retroactively, every person who held stock of *X* between January 1 and March 10 must consent to the election. *A* held stock from January 1 to his death on January 20. Obviously, *A* is not able to execute a consent on or after March 10. The question is whether *A*'s executor can consent on *A*'s behalf. In Rev. Rul. 92–82, the Commissioner ruled that an executor can consent on behalf of a deceased shareholder. So, the election will apply retroactively provided that the executor consents on behalf of both *A* and *A*'s estate.

Stock held by a custodian for a minor under the Uniform Transfers to Minors Act or the Uniform Gift to Minors Act is deemed owned by the minor and not by a trust—that is, the custodial arrangement is a type of informal guardianship and does not constitute a trust. See Rev. Rul. 71–287; PLR 8819011. Thus, even a corporate custodian can hold stock in an electing corporation without disqualifying its Subchapter S election. See Treas. Reg. § 1.1361–1(e)(1). However, for a shareholder who is a minor, the consent to a Subchapter S election must be made either by the minor himself, his legal guardian, or by a natural or adoptive parent if no legal guardian has been appointed. Treas. Reg. § 1.1362–6(b)(2)(ii). In Rev. Rul 66–116, as amplified by Rev. Rul. 68–227, the Commissioner ruled that a custodian of stock held for a minor cannot make a valid consent for the minor to a Subchapter S election unless the custodian happens also to be the minor's legal guardian or, if no legal guardian has been appointed, is the minor's natural or adoptive parent. This requirement could prove a trap for the unwary.

CHAPTER 3

EFFECT OF AN S ELECTION

§ 1. In General

A valid Subchapter S election does not eliminate the electing corporation as an entity for tax purposes. It does, however, relieve the corporation from federal income tax liability for most tax items. Subject to four exceptions (one of which is nearly obsolete), an S corporation is not subject to federal income taxation and instead serves as a conduit whose tax attributes are passed through to its shareholders. One of those exceptions occurs when a C corporation that uses the LIFO (last in-first out) method to account for its inventory becomes an S corporation. See Section 2(g) of Chapter 9. A second occurs when an S corporation recaptures an investment credit that was taken by the corporation when it was a C corporation; in that event, the corporation (rather than its shareholders) will be liable for the recapture of the tax credit. § 1371(d)(2). Third, in certain circumstances, all or part of an S corporation's recognized gains that are attributable to appreciation that took place at a time when the corporation was a C corporation (or took place while the property was held by another corporation that was a C corporation) will be taxed to the S corporation under § 1374. A fourth circumstance in which a federal income tax is imposed on an S corporation is where the corporation is subjected to a tax on passive investment income under § 1375. The latter two of those exceptions are explained in Chapters Eight and Nine, infra.

Also, as will be explained later, in certain circumstances, a corporation's taxable year can be divided into two parts, in one of which it will be an S corporation and in the other it will be a C corporation. See Section 6 of Chapter 7, infra. Of course, the corporation will be subject to federal income taxation on that amount of its income that is attributable to the portion of the year that it is a C corporation.

With two exceptions, all elections affecting the computation of tax items of an S corporation are made by the corporation. For example, the choice of a method of depreciation for the depreciable assets of the corporation and the decision whether to elect nonrecognition under § 1033 for gain recognized from the involuntary conversion of the corporation's assets are to be made by the corporation. The two tax elections that are made by the shareholders (as contrasted to the corporation) are listed in § 1363(c)(2) and apply to the foreign tax credit and the tax treatment of certain mining expenditures.

When a corporation that had received an investment tax credit when it was a C corporation subsequently becomes an S corporation, the Subchapter S election does not trigger a recapture of the credit that was previously taken. If all or a portion of the previously taken investment credit subsequently is recaptured by the S corporation under §§ 49(b) or 50, the S corporation (as contrasted to its shareholders) is liable for the tax. The tax paid by an S corporation because of a recapture of an investment tax credit reduces its earnings and profits, if any. § 1371(d). Since the 1986 TRA substantially reduced the scope of the investment tax credit, the provisions in Subchapter S that deal with that credit are of diminished consequence.

§ 2. Taxable Year

An S corporation's taxable year is restricted to a calendar year unless the corporation can establish a business purpose for using a different accounting period. § 1378(b).

The Revenue Act of 1987 added § 444 to the Code to permit certain entities, including S corporations, to elect a fiscal year as their taxable year in certain circumstances when that fiscal year would otherwise not be permitted. To make this election, the entity must make the payments required by § 7519; these payments essentially constitute an interest-free loan from the entity to the government.

§ 3. Pass–Through of Tax Items

The taxable income of an S corporation is computed in a similar manner to the computation of a partnership's taxable income, but there are some differences. While § 1363(b) states that an S corporation's taxable income is computed in the same manner as an individual's, that provision and § 1366(a) divide the S corporation's income into separate categories in a manner that is similar to the division of a partnership's income; and an S corporation is denied the same deductions that are denied to a partnership by § 703(a)(2) (a partnership provision). Those items of corporate income (including tax-exempt income), losses, deductions (including charitable contributions) and credits, the separate treatment of which could affect a shareholder's liability, are separately stated and allocated among the shareholders; for convenience, those items are referred to as "separately stated items." The balance of the corporation's taxable income or loss (which is determined by excluding all of the "separately stated items") is also allocated among the shareholders; this figure is referred to as the "nonseparately computed income or loss."

§ 1366(a). While §§ 1363(b)(2) and 703(a)(2)(C) deny an S corporation a deduction for its charitable contributions, its charitable contributions pass through to its shareholders who can take a deduction for them subject to the limitations imposed by § 170 on deductions allowable for charitable contributions.

The "pass-thru" of tax items for the taxable year of an S corporation is made to each shareholder for his taxable year in which the taxable year of the S corporation ends (or the final year of a shareholder who dies or of a trust or estate that terminates during the corporation's taxable year). This conduit aspect of an S corporation is sometimes referred to as a "pass-thru" of tax items, and that term is also used for partnerships. All of the S corporation's tax items are allocated among its shareholders on a daily basis. §§ 1366(a)(1), 1377. The reason for the "one class of stock" requirement is to simplify that allocation.

Subject to two exceptions, the character of any item of the S corporation's income, loss, deduction or credit that pass through to the shareholders is determined at the corporate level rather than by reference to the shareholders. Treas. Reg. § 1.1366–1(b). The two exceptions apply when a shareholder contributed to the S corporation either non-capital gain property or capital loss property if (and only if) the S corporation was formed or availed of for the principal purpose of selling or exchanging the property that if sold by the shareholder would have produced a gain or loss of a different character. Id.

Deductions, losses and credits that pass through to a shareholder are subject to the limitations on their deduction or application imposed by both the at risk rules of § 465 and the passive activity loss and credit limitation rules of § 469. Those limitations are applied to each shareholder rather than to the S corporation itself. There is an order of priority for the application of the several limitations on the deduction of pass-thru losses. First, the basis limitation rules are applied. Next the at risk limitations of § 465 are applied to whatever amount was allowed by the basis rules. Lastly, whatever amount has passed muster through the basis and at risk limitations then is subjected to the passive activity loss limitation rules. See Section 4 of Chapter 5, infra.

There are some tax items that are determined differently for an S corporation than would be the case for a partnership. For example, the deduction under § 248 that is allowed a corporation for organization expenses applies to an S corporation. Also, the special recapture and other corporate preference rules of § 291 apply to an S corporation if it (or a predecessor) had been a C corporation in any one of the three preceding taxable years. § 1363(b).

§ 4. Tax Returns and Consistency Requirement

An S corporation is required to file a tax return showing, among other items, its gross income and deductions, the names of its shareholders and their stock holdings at all times during the taxable year, the amount and date of distributions made to shareholders during the year, and each shareholder's pro rata share of each tax item of the corporation. § 6037(a). The corporation is required to furnish each shareholder a copy of the information on the corporation's return that the shareholder may need to know for reporting purposes. § 6037(b). In some circumstances, an S corporation is required to file its return on magnetic media. Treas. Reg. § 301.6037–2T.

On the tax return of each shareholder, the shareholder must treat "Subchapter S items" in a manner that is consistent with the treatment reported on the S corporation's tax return; or the shareholder must notify the Commissioner by filing a statement identifying any inconsistency of treatment. § 6037(c). A "Subchapter S item" is one that the regulations provide is more appropriately characterized at the corporate level than at the shareholder level. § 6037(c)(4).

§ 5. Reallocation Among Family Members

Since the federal income tax system utilizes graduated rates, there can be a tax advantage to splitting income away from a taxpayer in a high tax bracket to someone in a low tax bracket. Over the years, many devices have been employed to attempt to accomplish that income splitting. Many were determined to be unsuccessful by judicial decisions, primarily utilizing the anticipatory assignment of income principle; and Congress has adopted a number of provisions to prevent that from occurring.

One device that was utilized was to create a partnership between a high bracket taxpayer and one or more low bracket relatives, and then claim that the partnership's income is divided among the partners according to their percentage interests. For example, a parent could transfer his sole proprietorship to a partnership in which he and his minor children are partners. The results of those attempts were mixed. Congress addressed this problem by adopting § 704(e), which is aimed at family partnerships. Section 704(e) "essentially codifies assignment-of-income principles and provides special rules for (i) determining the status of a person as a partner and (ii) reallocating income between" the donors and donees of partnership interests. Karen C. Burke, "Federal Income Taxation of Partners and Partnerships," at pp. 168–169 (Thomson/West, 2005).

Since an S corporation is also a pass-through organization, taxpayers could attempt to utilize the S corporation form to split income among family members. To address that device, Congress adopted § 1366(e), which is a family shareholder rule that is roughly comparable to the family partnership rule mentioned above.

Under § 1366(e), if an individual who is a member of the family (as defined in § 704(e)(3)) of one or more shareholders of an S corporation renders services or furnishes capital to the corporation without receiving adequate compensation, the Commissioner is authorized to make appropriate adjustments in the items allocated to such individual and to the appropriate shareholders as may be necessary to reflect the value of those services or capital. The family of an individual includes only the spouse, ancestors, and lineal descendants of that individual, and any trusts for the primary benefit of such persons. The Commissioner, and only the Commissioner, is authorized by § 1366(e) to reallocate the corporation's items; neither the corporation nor its shareholders can initiate such a reallocation. Johnson v. Commissioner, 720 F.2d 963 (7th Cir. 1983).

§ 6.   Adjustment of Corporation's Tax Items

In computing the corporation's taxable income, those deductions that are described in § 703(a)(2) (e.g., personal exemptions, net operating losses, charitable contributions, depletion for oil and gas) are disallowed; but the deduction provided by § 248 for organizational expenses is allowed. The restrictive provisions of § 291, which reduce the tax benefits available to a corporation for certain preference items, will be applied in determining the taxable income of an S corporation for a taxable year if the S corporation (or a predecessor) had been a C corporation in any of the three preceding years. § 1363(b). This latter provision is designed to prevent a C corporation's escape from § 291 treatment by making a Subchapter S election a few years prior to incurring the § 291 item.

Note that while charitable contributions and depletion allowances for oil and gas are not deductible by the corporation, those items are passed through to the corporation's shareholders as separately stated items and thus may be deducted by the shareholders. §§ 613A(c)(11), 1366(a)(1); Treas. Reg. § 1.1366–1(a)(2)(iii).

§ 7.   Carryovers and Carrybacks

With one exception, no carryover or carryback arising in a taxable year of a C corporation can be carried to a year in which that corporation is an S corporation; but the S corporation year is counted as an elapsed year in determining the number of years to which an item can be carried forward or back. § 1371(b). The one exception is that a net operating loss carryover and a capital loss carryover from a C corporation year can be utilized in a subsequent S corporation year as a deduction against the S corporation's "net recognized built-in gain" for that year. § 1374(b)(2). The term "net recognized built-in gain" is defined in § 1374(d)(2)(A) and is discussed in Chapter 9, infra. Note that only such carry*over* losses can be utilized; a loss cannot be carried back to a prior S corporation year.

Except for disallowed losses and deductions that are carried forward pursuant to § 1366(d)(2) and (3), which provisions are explained in Sections 1 and 2 of Chapter 5, there is no carryover or carryback of an item that is incurred by a corporation in a year in which it is an S corporation. § 1371(b)(2). Since losses, credits and deductions of an S corporation pass through to the corporation's shareholders and are deducted or taken by them in their individual capacity, there is no reason to permit the corporation to carry forward or back its tax items. It is only when a shareholder is prevented, by not having adequate basis, from taking a deduction for an S corporation's loss that the corporation's loss can be carried forward to its next taxable year and then only with respect to that shareholder. § 1366(d). The one exception to the limitation making the carryover loss personal to the shareholder to whom the loss was allocated arises when that shareholder transfers stock to a spouse or former spouse in a transaction covered by § 1041(a); that exception is discussed in Section 1 of Chapter 5, infra. See Prop. Reg. § 1.1366–2(a)(5).

§ 8.   Character of Pass–Through Tax Items

The various tax items of an S corporation are passed through to its shareholders who report them as having the same characteristics as they have in the hands of the S corporation. § 1366(b). For example, capital gains and capital losses pass through as long-term or short-term depending upon the corporation's holding period. Similarly, tax-exempt income will pass through as such, and section 1231 gains and losses pass through as such.

§ 9.   Pass–Through of Built–In Gains and the Tax Thereon

One of the circumstances in which an S corporation will incur income tax liability is when it has so-called "built-in gains." § 1374. A built-in gain refers to income recognized by an S corporation that is attributable to appreciation or other unrecognized income that arose in the hands of what was then a C corporation and is subsequently recognized by a corporation when it is an S corporation. When recognized, such gains are referred to as "recognized built-in gains." Thus, the tax imposed by § 1374 will generally not apply to a corporation that has always been an S corporation and has not received any assets from a C corporation in a carryover basis transaction. Even then, as discussed in Chapter 9, the § 1374 tax applies only if the built-in gain is recognized within 10 years of the corporation's election to be an S corporation or within 10 years of its receipt of the assets from a C corporation in a carryover basis transaction.

The corporation's recognized built-in gains for a taxable year are netted with its recognized built-in losses, and the net figure, if positive, generally constitutes what is called the "net recognized built-in gain" for the year. While the amount of the corporation's net recognized built-in gain is subject to a ceiling in that it cannot exceed a modified version of the corporation's taxable income, that ceiling applies only for purposes of determining the tax imposed on the corporation for its net recognized built-in gain. There is no ceiling on the amount of recognized built-in gain that will pass through to the corporation's shareholders.

The operation of the provision taxing the S corporation on its net recognized built-in gain is discussed in Chapter 9, infra. In this chapter, we examine the manner in which the entire amount of the built-in gains and the income tax liability incurred by the S corporation on its net recognized built-in gain are passed through to the shareholders.

When a tax on the net recognized built-in gain of an S corporation is imposed by § 1374, the tax is treated as a loss sustained by the corporation in that year. The "loss" is characterized by allocating it proportionately among the recognized built-in gains that gave rise to the tax. § 1366(f)(2).

One consequence of this treatment is that the pass-thru of an S corporation's "built-in gains" for a taxable year to a shareholder effectively is reduced by the proportionate share of the taxes incurred by the corporation, pursuant to § 1374, on its net recognized built-in gain. However, characterizing the § 1374 tax as a loss can provide a different result in certain circumstances than would occur if the provision merely reduced the amount of pass-thru of the corporation's built-in gains by the amount of the § 1374 tax. The problem arises when the corporation's § 1374 tax for a year is greater than the aggregate of its built-in gains for that year that pass through to the shareholders. (That seemingly implausible result can occur, as described below, as a consequence of the rule that limits the net recognized built-in gain taxable in any year to the amount of taxable income that would be taxed to the corporation if it were a C corporation.) Since there is no provision permitting a pass-through of a negative amount when the § 1374 tax exceeds the net recognized built-in gain passed through to the shareholders, an offset treatment would leave the shareholder with no benefit from the excess § 1374 tax. By treating the § 1374 tax as a loss, it will pass through to the shareholders and be deductible by them.

Prior to 1989, § 1366(f)(2) provided only that the amount of the built-in gain that is passed through to shareholders be reduced by the amount of the § 1374 tax; the provision was amended in 1989 to characterize the tax as a loss. This amendment was designed to cure a problem that arose with merely reducing the pass-thru of built-in gains by the § 1374 tax because of a change made in the Technical and Miscellaneous Revenue Act of 1988 to the taxation of built-in gains when the corporation's taxable income is less than the amount of its net built-in gains. The 1988 amendment put a ceiling on the amount of a corporation's net recognized built-in gain so that it cannot exceed a modified version of the corporation's taxable income determined as if it were a C corporation. However, any recognized built-in gain that escaped taxation because of that limitation is carried over to and taxed to the corporation in succeeding years. § 1374(d)(2)(B).

Although this excess recognized built-in gain is carried over for purposes of the corporate-level § 1374 tax, it was still passed through to the shareholders in the year in which the built-in gain was recognized. As a result, in the carryover year when the remainder of the built-in gain is taxed to the S corporation under § 1374, the § 1374 tax may well exceed the amount of built-in gain that is passed through to the shareholders in such carryover year. If left unchanged, this result would be more onerous on the shareholders than if the S corporation were a C corporation, which was clearly an unintended result. This unintended consequence of the 1988 amendment was corrected by the 1989 amendment, which operates retroactively to 1988.

The following example illustrates the significance of the 1989 amendment. In this example, it is assumed that none of the limitations on a shareholder's deduction of a pass-thru loss is applicable.

Ex.   Z Corporation, which had been a C corporation, became an S corporation in 1989, and it has been an S corporation ever since. In 1989, Z recognized a built-in gain of $15,000 and had deductible expenses of $8,000. Z had no other income or deductions in that year and had no recognized built-in loss. As explained in Chapter 9, § 1374 imposes a tax (in 1989 and 1990, the tax was at a 34 percent rate; currently, it is at a 35% rate) on $7,000 of Z's income (the lesser of the net of Z's recognized built-in gains and losses or its taxable income). As a result, Z incurred a § 1374 tax of $2,380 for 1989. While Z was taxed on only $7,000 of its recognized built-in gain, the entire $15,000 of that gain was passed through to Z's shareholders and became taxable in their hands. In addition, the $2,380 § 1374 tax that Z incurred was passed through to Z's shareholders and treated as a deductible loss in their hands. § 1366(f)(2).

The $8,000 difference between Z's recognized built-in gain of $15,000 and its $7,000 of taxable income, which represents the amount of Z's 1989 recognized built-in gain that was not taxed to Z in that year, was carried over and treated as a recognized built-in gain in the following year (1990). § 1374(d)(2)(B). In 1990, apart from the $8,000 carryover described above, Z had a built-in gain of $1,000, income of $12,000 from a retail book business, and had no deductions. The § 1374 tax on that $1,000 of built-in gain was $340. In addition, because of the carryover, Z was treated as having another $8,000 of recognized built-in gain in 1990, and the § 1374 tax on that figure was $2,720 (34% x $8,000). Thus, the total built-in gain tax for 1990 was $3,060 ($2,720 + $340). But, the only built-in gain of Z that passed through to its shareholders was the $1,000 of *actual* built-in gain that Z had in that year. If the § 1374 tax were to serve only to reduce the amount of pass-thru built-in gain for 1990, only $1,000 of the $3,060 tax would be useful, and no relief would be provided for the payment of the remaining $2,060 of the tax. The 1989 amendment cured that problem. Since the amendment classifies the $3,060 tax as a loss incurred by Z, the entire amount of the tax passed through to Z's shareholders as a deductible item. The 1989 amendment operates retroactively as if it were part of the 1988 Act.

§ 10. Pass–Through of Passive Investment Income

In certain circumstances described in Chapter 8, infra, a corporation is taxed at a 35 percent rate on an adjusted amount of its passive investment income. The tax is imposed on what is called the "excess net passive income." However, all of the corporation's passive investment income, not merely its excess net passive income, passes through to the shareholders and is included in their income.

Under § 1366(f)(3), the pass-thru of an S corporation's passive investment income to a shareholder is reduced by the proportionate share of the tax that the corporation incurred pursuant to § 1375. Unlike the § 1374 tax, there was no need to characterize this tax as a loss because the tax cannot exceed the amount of the corporation's passive investment income for that year.

The taxes imposed by §§ 1374 and 1375 on an S corporation's net recognized built-in gain and excess net passive income respectively are discussed in Chapters Eight and Nine, infra.

§ 11. Earnings and Profits

A corporation will not accumulate any earnings and profits (*"e and p"*) that arise from earnings that it has in a year in which it is an S corporation. § 1371(c)(1). There are two situations that can cause an S corporation to have accumulated *e and p*. An S corporation can have accumulated *e and p* if: it accumulated the *e and p* in a year when it was a C corporation; or it inherited the *e and p* of another corporation that the S corporation acquired pursuant to either a § 368 reorganization or a § 332 liquidation of a controlled subsidiary corporation. A "reorganization" is a term of art in the tax area that refers to certain corporate amalgamations, structural adjustments or divisions that satisfy specified requirements and generally qualify for nonrecognition treatment.

When an S corporation does possess accumulated *e and p*, its *e and p* will be reduced for its distributions to a shareholder to the extent that the distributions are treated as dividend income to the shareholder under § 1368(c)(2). See Chapter 6 for a discussion of when a distribution from an S corporation can be a dividend. The corporation's *e and p* also will be adjusted because of reorganizations, stock redemptions, corporate divisions, and liquidations in the same manner as if the corporation were a C corporation. § 1371(c)(2). If an S corporation incurs a tax liability for the recapture of an investment credit that was taken in a prior year when it was a C corporation, the amount of that tax liability will reduce the S corporation's *e and p*. § 1371(d)(3).

CHAPTER 4

SHAREHOLDER'S BASIS IN S CORPORATION'S STOCK AND DEBT OBLIGATIONS

§ 1. Adjustments to Shareholder's Basis

A shareholder's basis in stock of an S corporation usually is determined under the same rules that are generally applicable to the determination of basis of other items. However, there are a few circumstances in which specific rules apply.

A donee can have two different bases in property received as a gift if the donor's basis was greater than the property's value at the time of the gift. Under § 1015(a), for purposes of determining the donee's *loss* on a subsequent disposition of the property, the donee's basis is different from the basis that the donee has for determining gain. In such cases, for purposes of applying the stock basis limitation on the deduction of pass–thru losses (see section 1 of chapter 5), Treas. Reg. § 1.1366–2(a)(6) provides that the donee's *loss* basis for stock of an S corporation will be used.

If a shareholder acquires S stock on the death of a prior shareholder, the current shareholder's basis is determined under § 1014. However, § 1367(b)(4) requires that the current shareholder's basis be reduced by his share of items of the corporation that would be "income in respect of a decedent" under § 691 if such items had been held by the prior shareholder at the time of his death.

The most significant special treatment for the basis of the stock of an S corporation is the adjustments that are made to that basis. Under § 1367, a shareholder's basis in his stock in an S corporation is adjusted to reflect the corporation's items that have been allocated to that shareholder—e.g., his stock basis is increased by his share of the corporation's income items (including tax-exempt income) and by his share of the excess of depletion deductions over the basis of the depletable property; and his stock basis is reduced (but not below zero) by his share of losses, deductions, non-capital expenses that are not deductible, the amount of oil and gas depletion deduction that does not exceed the shareholder's proportionate share of the adjusted basis of the depletable property, and by § 301 distributions received from the corporation and not included in the shareholder's income under § 1368. A § 301 distribution is described in § 301 of the Code as property that a corporation distributes to a shareholder with respect to the shareholder's stock in the distributing corporation. See Chapter 6 for a discussion of the treatment of distributions made to a shareholder. The corporation's capital expenditures will not affect a shareholder's basis in the corporation's stock; however, a shareholder's share of deductions allowed for the amortization or depreciation of the asset that was acquired by the corporation will reduce the shareholder's basis. A loss that passes through to a shareholder will reduce the shareholder's basis in the corporation's stock regardless of whether the shareholder derives a tax benefit from deducting the loss. For example, if a loss that passes through to a shareholder cannot be deducted by the shareholder that year because of the limitations imposed either by the at risk rules of § 465 or the passive activity loss rules of § 469, the shareholder's basis nevertheless will be reduced. If, in a subsequent year, the shareholder is permitted to deduct the disallowed item, the shareholder's basis is not affected by that deduction since it was reduced when the loss passed through.

The adjustments to stock basis are made on a per share, per day basis. Treas. Reg. § 1.1367–1(b)(2), (c)(3). The adjustments generally are made as of the end of the corporation's taxable year, and are effective as of that date. However, if a shareholder disposes of any of a corporation's stock during the corporation's taxable year, the shareholder's basis in that stock will be adjusted immediately prior to the disposition, and that adjustment can affect the shareholder's gain or loss from that disposition. Treas. Reg. § 1.1367–1(d)(1).

A shareholder's basis in a share of stock cannot be reduced below zero; but, if the amount of reduction attributable to a share exceeds the share's basis, the excess is applied to reduce (but not below zero) the remaining bases of the shareholder's other shares of the corporation's stock in proportion to the remaining basis of each of those shares. Treas. Reg. § 1.1367–1(c)(3). If the total amount of basis reductions that are caused by an allocation of items to a shareholder's shares of stock (exclusive of reductions of basis that are attributable to the shareholder's receipt of distributions from the corporation) exceeds the aggregate basis of the shareholder's shares of stock, the excess is applied to reduce the shareholder's basis (but not below zero) in any indebtedness of the corporation that the shareholder holds at the close of the corporation's taxable year. § 1367(b)(2)(A); Treas. Reg. § 1.1367–2(b)(1). The apparent reason for reducing the basis of stock before reducing the basis of a debt is to minimize the situations when a shareholder will recognize income from collecting on the debt.

A net increase (i.e., the excess of the positive adjustments allocable to that shareholder over the negative adjustments) in a subsequent year with respect to the shareholder shall first be applied to restore the shareholder's basis in such debt to the extent that it was reduced in prior years, and only after the reductions of a shareholder's basis in such debt are fully restored can the basis of the shareholder's stock be increased. Treas. Reg. § 1.1367–2(c).

Ex. (1)   Individual *A* is the sole shareholder of *X* Corporation. As of January 1, Year One, *A* had a basis of $10,000 in his 100 shares of *X*'s stock, and *A* had a basis of $4,000 in a promissory note that evidences a debt that *X* owes to *A*. At all relevant times in this example, *X* is an S corporation that reports its income on a calendar year basis; and *X* has no earnings and profits. In Year One, *X* had a loss of $13,000. *X* made no distributions to its shareholder in that year. The $13,000 loss passes through to *A* and is deductible by him, subject to the limitation on deductions. Even if *A* were prevented from deducting the loss because of the limitations imposed by § 465 or § 469, *A*'s basis would still be reduced. *A*'s basis in his 100 shares of *X*'s stock is reduced from $10,000 to zero. *A*'s basis in the promissory note of *X* is reduced from $4,000 to $1,000. In Year Two, *X* had $2,000 of net income (after taking into account all items of gross income and deductible expenses), and *X* made no distributions to its shareholder. *A* will include the corporation's $2,000 of income in his tax return for Year Two. *A*'s basis in his 100 shares of *X*'s stock will continue to be zero, but A's basis in the promissory note will be increased to $3,000. In Year Three, X had net income of $3,500, all of which passes through to A, and X made no distributions to A in that year. A's basis in the promissory note is increased to $4,000, and A has a basis of $2,500 in his 100 shares of X's stock.

Ex. (2)   The same facts as those stated in **Ex. (1)**. In Year Four, X had neither a gain nor a loss. In that year, X distributed $4,500 cash to A, its sole shareholder. As discussed later, since X had no earnings and profits and since the distribution exceeds A's basis in his X stock by $2,000, A will recognize income of $2,000 from the distribution. § 1368(b)(2). A's basis in his X stock will be reduced to zero. A's basis in the promissory note will continue to be $4,000.

The basis adjustments to stock provided by § 1367 are similar to the adjustments made to a partner's basis in his partnership interest under § 705. Note, however, that there is no counterpart in Subchapter S for § 752, which increases a partner's basis in his partnership interest for his share of partnership liabilities. An S corporation's liabilities do not increase a shareholder's basis in his stock. Note also that there is no provision in partnership taxation for a reduction of a partner's basis in partnership debt because of an allocation of the partnership's tax items.

As discussed in Section 1 of Chapter 5, infra, the amount of net loss that passes through to a shareholder from an S corporation can be deducted only to the extent of the shareholder's basis in both the corporation's stock and in debt that the corporation owed to the shareholder. § 1366(d)(1). In addition, the deduction is limited by the at risk rules and passive activity loss limitations of §§ 465 and 469. Under § 1366(d)(2), any loss that cannot be deducted by the shareholder because of the § 1366(d) limitation is carried over by the corporation indefinitely as a loss that is allocable to that shareholder. Such a carryover loss is sometimes referred to as a "§ 1366(d) loss." Subject to the at risk limitation of § 465 and the passive activity loss limitation of § 469, the shareholder can deduct such carryover losses in subsequent years to the extent that the shareholder then has a basis in his stock or debt. While this § 1366(d) carryover loss typically is personal to the shareholder who was denied the deduction because of inadequate basis, there is one circumstance where the right to deduct the loss can be transferred to another. If the shareholder on whose behalf the corporation's loss is carried over transfers any of his stock to a spouse or former spouse in a transaction that qualifies for § 1041(a) treatment, the carryover loss with respect to that stock will be treated as incurred by the corporation in the next year with respect to the transferee. § 1366(d)(2)(B).

When a debt is forgiven, the debtor will recognize income in the amount forgiven unless one of a number of exceptions is applicable. Some of the exceptions are judicially created, but many are set forth in § 108 of the Code. One especially important exception is that a debtor will not recognize income to the extent that the debtor was insolvent immediately prior to the forgiveness of the debt. When the debtor is an S corporation, insolvency is to be determined at the corporate level rather than by referring to the solvency of the shareholders. § 108(a), (d)(7). The amount that is excluded from a debtor's income under the insolvency exception typically will cause a reduction of specified favorable tax attributes that the debtor possesses (including net operating losses), but will not do so if the debtor does not possess any of those tax attributes. In the case of the cancellation of a debt of an S corporation, it is the tax attributes of the S corporation that will be reduced by the unrecognized income; and any carryover § 1366(d) losses that the corporation possesses are treated as a net operating loss for that purpose. § 108(d)(7)(A), (B).

The question arose as to the proper treatment of the circumstance where an insolvent S corporation had cancellation of indebtedness that was excluded from income by the insolvency provision of § 108(a)(1). Should that unrecognized income pass through to the shareholders and increase their basis in their corporate stock even though the pass-thru item was not taxable to them because of the insolvency exception? The exclusion of the item from the shareholder's income does not depend upon their solvency since the insolvency standard is applied at the corporate level.

The Commissioner took the position that the unrecognized cancellation of indebtedness income does not increase a shareholder's basis in his stock. Before the Supreme Court passed on that issue, the results of litigating it were mixed. In Gitlitz v. Commissioner, 531 U.S. 206 (2001), the Supreme Court held that the unrecognized cancellation of indebtedness income does increase the shareholders' basis in their stock.

In *Gitlitz*, the two shareholders of the insolvent S corporation had a zero basis in their stock. The corporation had a substantial carryover loss under § 1366(d) that was allocable to the two shareholders. The corporation had a large amount of debt forgiven, and none of it was taxable because of the corporation's insolvency. The taxpayer contended that the unrecognized income was comparable to tax-exempt income, which the Code expressly provides passes through to the shareholders and increases their basis in their stock. With the increased basis, the shareholders claimed that they could then deduct the corporation's § 1366(d) carryover loss that is allocable to them. While, under § 108(b), the corporation's § 1366(d) carryover loss would be reduced by the unrecognized income from the cancellation of indebtedness, the shareholders contended that the income allocation and basis adjustment take place before the carryover loss is reduced. The Supreme Court held for the taxpayer and allowed them to increase their basis in their stock and take a deduction for the carryover loss that was allocable to them.

A number of commentators severely criticized the Supreme Court's decision in *Gitlitz*. In 2002, Congress repudiated the result reached in *Gitlitz* by amending § 108(d)(7)(A) to exclude from items that pass through to shareholders under § 1366(a) any amount excluded from the S corporation's income by § 108(a). Thus, an S corporation's cancellation of indebtedness income that is not taxed because of the insolvency exception does not pass through to shareholders and so does not affect the basis in their stock.

§ 2.   Order of Adjustments and Effect on Shareholder's Deduction of Loss and Treatment of Receipt of Corporate Distributions

When several separate events cause adjustments to be made to a shareholder's basis in stock of an S corporation or in debt of the corporation that is owed to the shareholder, the order in which the adjustments are to be made can be important.

Ex.   In Year One, S corporation, which has no accumulated earnings and profits, had a capital gain of $500 and an ordinary loss of $800. On the last day of that same taxable year, the corporation made a distribution of $250 cash to its sole shareholder, who holds no debt of the corporation and who had a basis of $400 in the corporation's stock at the beginning of the year. The shareholder's basis in the stock will be increased by the $500 gain, decreased by the $800 ordinary loss, and decreased by the $250 cash distribution, subject to the limitation that his basis cannot be reduced below zero. The order in which those increases and decreases in basis take place will determine the extent to which the shareholder can deduct the pass-thru loss of the S corporation and the extent (if any) to which the cash distribution will cause the shareholder to recognize income. The order of adjustments to basis is explained below.

The order of adjustments is set forth in Treas. Reg. § 1.1367–1(f). According to that regulation, the adjustments to stock basis are made in the following order:

 (1) first, basis of stock is increased by its share of the corporation's income (including tax-exempt income) and by its

share of the excess of depletion deductions over the basis of depletable property;

(2) next, basis of stock is reduced by § 301 distributions received by the shareholder that year from the corporation that are not included in the shareholder's income under § 1368;

(3) next, basis of stock is reduced for its share of non-capital, nondeductible expenses, and for its share of the oil and gas depletion deduction that does not exceed its share of the adjusted basis of the depletable property;

(4) finally, basis of stock is reduced for its share of losses and deductions.

A shareholder may elect under Treas. Reg. § 1.1367–1(g) to reverse the order of items (3) and (4) above. Once a shareholder makes that election, the shareholder must continue to use that ordering system in subsequent years unless the Commissioner permits a change.

Referring to the example set forth above, the shareholder's $400 basis in the corporation's stock first is increased by the corporation's $500 capital gain. The shareholder therefore had a stock basis of $900 to utilize against the $250 distribution, and so the shareholder did not recognize any income from receiving that distribution. The shareholder's stock basis then would be reduced by the $250 cash distribution that the shareholder received from the corporation, leaving the shareholder an adjusted basis of $650 to utilize in determining the extent to which the shareholder can deduct the $800 corporate loss that passes through to the shareholder. The shareholder can deduct $650 of that $800 loss, and the remaining $150 of that loss is carried forward to the next year under § 1366(d)(2).

The shareholder will include the $500 of the corporation's capital gain in his income (as pass-thru capital gain income) and will deduct $650 of the $800 ordinary loss that passes through to him.

The shareholder's basis in his stock, for purposes of determining the amount of loss deduction he is permitted, is determined at the end of the taxable year before taking into account the corporation's losses. § 1366(d)(1)(A). So, for that purpose, the shareholder had a basis of $650 in the stock (i.e., the $400 basis that the shareholder had at the beginning of the year plus the $500 capital gain that passes through to him minus the $250 distribution that was not taxable income to him). As noted above, the shareholder can deduct $650 of the $800 corporate loss, and the remaining $150 is carried forward to the next year under § 1366(d)(2). Of course, any deduction by the shareholder is subject to the limitations imposed by §§ 465 and 469.

In the above illustration, the cash distribution did not constitute a dividend to the shareholder because the corporation had no *e and p*. In determining the effect of the shareholder's receipt of the cash distribution, it is necessary to determine the basis that the shareholder had in the corporation's stock so that the amount (if any) of the distribution that constitutes a gain can be calculated. For this purpose, the shareholder's basis in the stock will reflect the adjustments required because of the corporation's income that passes through to the shareholder but without regard to corporate losses. Since the shareholder had enough basis in his stock ($400) at the beginning of the year to prevent the $250 distribution from causing a gain, there is no need in this case to determine how much adjustment to his basis because of the corporation's income is available to the distribution. Also, since the distribution was made on the last day of the taxable year, all of the corporation's income for that year would adjust the shareholder's basis before determining whether the distribution caused him to recognize income. Clearly, the shareholder did not recognize income.

Let us change the facts of the example so that the $250 distribution was made on February 1, Year One, and the shareholder's basis in his stock at the beginning of the year was zero. The consequence of the shareholder's receipt of the distribution on February 1 turns on how

much of the corporation's income adjusts the
shareholder's basis in his stock at the time he
received the distribution. If all $500 of the
income that the corporation had in that taxable
year is used, the shareholder will not recognize
any gain from the distribution. But, if only a
prorated amount of the corporation's income
(1/12 of $500 = $41.67) is used to adjust the
shareholder's stock at the time that he received
the $250 distribution, the shareholder will rec-
ognize income. Which of those alternatives is
correct?

There is a suggestion in the legislative history of the 1982 SRA that the shareholder's basis
is adjusted for the income of the corporation
for the entire taxable year before the tax consequence of the distribution is determined. Both
the Senate Finance Committee's Report and
the House Ways and Means Committee's Report for the 1982 SRA state (S. Rep. No. 640,
97th Cong., 2d Sess. 18 (1982); H.R. Rep. No.
826, 97th Cong., 2d Sess. 17 (1982)):

> Under the bill, both taxable and nontaxable
> income will serve to increase a Subchapter S
> shareholder's basis in the stock of the corpo-
> ration. These rules generally will be analo-
> gous to those provided for partnerships un-
> der section 705. Under these rules, income
> for any corporate taxable year will apply to
> adjust basis before the distribution rules ap-
> ply for that year.

While the reference in the legislative history to "income for any corporate taxable year" does not necessarily mean that *all* of the corporation's income for the taxable year should be utilized rather than limiting the adjustments to a pro rata portion of such income, the language does suggest the former meaning. A competing consideration is that an apparent purpose of the provision was to approximate for S corporations the treatment accorded to partnerships by § 705, and it appears that the effect of a distribution from a partnership to a partner (other than a distribution that constitutes an advance or draw against the partner's share of partnership profits for that year) is determined by adjusting the partner's basis in his partnership interest only for partnership income that is allocable to the partner's interest for the period preceding the distribution. Nevertheless, while the issue is unsettled, the authors believe that the more likely construction is to adjust basis for the entire year's corporate income.

§ 3. Shareholder's Guaranty of Third–Party's Loan to Corporation

When a loan is made to an S corporation by a financial institution (or by some other third party) and when the repayment of the loan is guaranteed by one or more of the borrower's shareholders, in a number of cases those share-holders have sought to invoke the substance versus form doctrine to recast the transaction as a loan made directly from the financial institution to the shareholders who then are deemed either to contribute the loan proceeds to the S corporation or to have loaned the proceeds to that corporation. If the transaction can be so recast, the shareholder-guarantors either would increase their basis in their stock by their share of the loan proceeds or they would have that amount of basis in a debt owing to them by the S corporation. Such an increase in stock basis or in the shareholder's basis in corporate debt would increase the amount of the shareholder's allocable share of corporate losses that the shareholder can de-duct.

While this issue has been raised in a number of cases, the shareholders were successful in only one case, and that case rested on a distinc-tive set of facts.

All of the courts agree that a shareholder must have incurred an economic outlay to ob-tain basis in either stock or debt of an S corporation. However, in a 1985 decision of the Eleventh Circuit in Selfe v. United States, 778 F.2d 769, the court held that the substance versus form doctrine could be employed to treat a guarantee of a loan to the corporation as an economic outlay. Every court thereafter that has passed on this issue has declined to apply the substance versus form doctrine on the facts presented in those cases. Even the Eleventh Circuit itself, in a subsequent decision, noted that the facts of *Selfe* are unusual, and held that in the more usual situation, a guarantor will not thereby acquire basis in the corporation's stock or debt. Sleiman v. Commissioner, 187 F.3d 1352 (11th Cir. 1999).

In *Selfe*, the taxpayer, who was an individual, gave security to a bank for a line of credit to borrow money to provide funds for a retail clothing business that she had begun. Shortly thereafter, the business was incorporated as an S corporation, and the bank requested that the loans then outstanding be converted to a loan to the corporation. The bank retained the security that the taxpayer had provided, and the taxpayer executed an agreement guaranteeing the loan. While the corporation incurred losses, it never defaulted on the loan, and so taxpayer never made any payments under her guarantee.

The taxpayer described herself as a novice in a fledgling business engaged in a competitive area. The corporation was said to be thinly capitalized. A deposition of the loan officer of the bank stated that the bank primarily looked to the taxpayer, and not to the corporation, for repayment of the loan.

The Service rejected the taxpayer's claim for a deduction for losses that passed through to her from the corporation because she did not have sufficient basis in her stock. Taxpayer sued for a refund in the District Court claiming that the loan from the bank was actually made to her and then contributed by her to the corporation so that it should be added to her basis in her stock. The District Court granted summary judgment for the government. The Eleventh Circuit reversed and held that there were material facts to be determined; and if the facts claimed by the taxpayer were found to be correct, she could obtain a basis in her stock. The court remanded the case to the District Court for further findings to determine whether the bank loan was in reality a loan to the taxpayer.

No other court has permitted a guarantee to provide basis for an S corporation's stock or debt. Apart from *Selfe*, every court that has passed on this issue has held that the substance versus form principle did not serve to provide the shareholder with basis. The prevailing rule is that a shareholder must incur an actual economic outlay to obtain basis; and in the circumstance of a guarantee, that generally means that the shareholder will get basis only for payments actually made on the debt by the shareholder. On the other hand, one frequently cited authority outside the S corporation context has held that a shareholder can be deemed to have made an economic outlay to the corporation when the facts reveal that the third party lender in fact relied on the credit of the shareholder, and not that of the corporation (as the lender was prepared to testify in the *Selfe* case), in extending the credit and that, as a consequence, the substance of the transaction was a loan from the lender to the shareholder followed by the shareholder reloaning the funds to the corporation. *Plantation Patterns, Inc. v. Commissioner*, 462 F.2d 712 (5th Cir. 1972). It was this case on which the Eleventh Circuit in *Selfe* relied in support of its holding that the shareholder in that case had in substance made the necessary economic outlay.

Nevertheless, the position taken by the Eleventh Circuit in *Selfe* has been rejected by the Tax Court and by the Courts of Appeals of five other circuits, although in most cases because the facts of those cases were found not to support the conclusion reached in *Plantation Patterns* and *Selfe* regarding the substance of the loan transaction. In a subsequent case, *Sleiman v. Commissioner*, 187 F.3d 1352 (11th Cir. 1999), the Eleventh Circuit itself distinguished *Selfe* on its facts because of the absence of persuasive evidence that the substance of the third-party financing was not a loan to the corporation but rather a loan to the shareholder followed by the shareholder's advancing the funds to the corporation.

This issue arises principally where the corporate borrower's assets are insufficient to qualify for the loan. In such cases, there can be reason to believe that the purported guarantors of the loan (the shareholders) in fact are the true borrowers. It is more plausible that the lender is looking to the "guarantors" as the parties who are primarily liable on the debt if the corporation is thinly capitalized. Where such "loans" have been made to a thinly capitalized C corporation, there is precedent, as noted above, for treating the loan as having been made to the shareholders and then contributed by them to the corporation. However, as also noted above, with the exception of the *Selfe* decision, the courts have uniformly declined, at least on the facts of the cases before them, to apply that approach in an S corporation context so as to find the necessary economic outlay that will provide basis in an S corporation's stock or debt.

There is another potential obstacle to a shareholder's succeeding in a claim that a purported loan to an S corporation was actually a loan to the shareholder. When a transaction is made in a specified manner by a taxpayer, the taxpayer generally will not be allowed to recast the transaction as being something else, or, at least, will have to satisfy a heavy burden of proof to do so. There is concern that a taxpayer should not be allowed to cast a transaction in one form, and then, if subsequent events make another form more desirable, raise the substance versus form principle to recast the transaction into a more favorable category. The assumption is that, since the taxpayer has the best knowledge of the facts, the question of the substance of the transaction likely will not be raised unless it proves advantageous to the taxpayer. If the taxpayer is allowed to recast a transaction, it gives him a kind of "heads I win and tails I win" situation—i.e., the taxpayer can leave the transaction as described if that proves more favorable and recast it if that turns out to be more favorable.

The question is to what extent can taxpayers utilize the substance versus form principle; there is no limitation on the government's use of the principle. Different courts have applied different standards for the circumstances in which a court will permit a taxpayer to recast a transaction to which the taxpayer was a party, and even the Internal Revenue Service is not consistent with respect to when taxpayers can apply the substance versus form principle, but rather takes the position that taxpayers can more readily apply it with respect to some tax issues than they can with respect to others. Some courts have cited such restrictions on taxpayer use of substance versus form as an alternative ground for denying the taxpayer's claim to increased basis of an S corporation's stock or debt. See e.g., Uri v. Commissioner, 949 F.2d 371 (10th Cir. 1991). One of the several judicial approaches to the question of the standard for permitting a taxpayer to repudiate the form of a contract of which the taxpayer was a party is referred to as the "Daniel-son" rule because of a Third Circuit decision by that name. Commissioner v. Danielson, 378 F.2d 771 (3d Cir. 1967) (en banc). The Daniel-son rule, which has not been uniformly adopted, imposes an especially heavy burden on a taxpayer to contradict the terms of a transaction of the taxpayer. In *Selfe,* the Eleventh Circuit noted that rule, but determined that it was not an absolute bar and that the taxpayer could use the substance versus form rule in the circumstances of that case.

CHAPTER 5

LIMITATIONS ON DEDUCTIONS

§ 1. In General

A shareholder can deduct a loss or deduction passed through to him from an S corporation only to the extent of his basis in the S corporation's stock and in any indebtedness owing to him from the corporation. As described in Section 2 of Chapter 4, for this purpose, the shareholder's basis in the S corporation's stock is determined at the end of the S corporation's taxable year after taking into account adjustments under § 1367(a)—e.g., positive adjustments for the sum of the shareholder's portion of the corporation's income and negative adjustments for items of loss and deductions that pass through to the shareholders.

A loss or deduction that is disallowed to a shareholder because of inadequate basis is carried forward with the same character and treated as a loss or deduction incurred by the corporation in the succeeding year with respect to that shareholder. § 1366(d)(2)(A). Thus, the shareholder can utilize the loss or deduction in a later year in which he has a basis in his stock or debt. This treatment is similar to the treatment accorded to partners by § 704(d) except that partners are not permitted to utilize their basis in partnership debt instruments to qualify for deductions allocated to them.

A loss carried forward to a subsequent year is sometimes referred to as a "§ 1366(d) loss." The character of the loss deduction that passes through to a shareholder is determined by allocating the deduction proportionately among the corporation's deductible items for that year. Treas. Reg. § 1.1366–2(a)(4). Similarly, the character of the § 1366(d) loss that is carried forward is determined by making a proportional allocation among the corporation's deductible items.

Prop. Reg. § 1.1366–2(a)(5) states, with one exception, that the carryover of a disallowed § 1366(d) loss is personal to the shareholder to whom that loss was allocated, and cannot be transferred to another person. The one exception was created by a 2004 amendment adopting § 1366(d)(2)(B). That amendment applies when a shareholder who has rights to a carryover § 1366(d) loss transfers stock to a spouse (or to a former spouse) in a transaction covered by § 1041(a). Beginning with the next taxable year, the carryover § 1366(d) loss that was attributable to the transferor will be deemed to have been incurred by the corporation with respect to the transferee. If a shareholder transfers only a portion of his stock to a spouse or former spouse in a § 1041(a) transaction, only a portion of the carryover § 1366(d) loss that had been attributable to the transferor will be available to the transferee; and the remaining portion of the carryover loss will continue to be available to the transferor. Prop. Reg. § 1.1366–2(a)(5) describes how that allocation is made.

In our subsequent discussion of the operation of the § 1366(d) carryover loss, we will concentrate on situations that do not invoke the exception for § 1041(a) transactions. For convenience, to designate transferees of stock who do not qualify for the exception for § 1041(a) transferees, we will refer to such a transferee or donee as a "non-spouse" transferee or donee.

Thus, for example, a non-spouse donee of all of a shareholder's stock will not acquire the donor's right to a § 1366(d) carryover loss; and the carryover § 1366(d) loss that was allocable to the donor is permanently disallowed. If a shareholder for whom a disallowed loss has been carried forward transfers some of his stock to a non-spouse donee and retains the rest, the amount of the donor's right to the carryover of a § 1366(d) loss is not diminished; the donor continues to have the same right to deduct that carryover § 1366(d) loss when the donor has basis in the corporation's stock or debt. Treas. Reg. § 1.1366–2(a)(5).

In the examples below, it is assumed that the limitations in § 465 (the at risk rules) and § 469 (the passive activity loss rules) do not deny a deduction to the shareholder. However, even if those limitations applied to prevent the shareholder from deducting all or part of the pass-thru losses, the shareholder's basis in the corporation's stock and debt would be reduced by the full amount of the pass-thru loss.

Ex. (1)   *Y* Corporation is an S corporation that reports its income on a calendar year basis. *B* owns all 100 shares of *Y*'s outstanding stock, and *B* owns a promissory note of *Y* evidencing *Y*'s debt to *B* of $3,000. *B* reports her income on a calendar year basis. As of January 1, Year One, *B* had a basis of $8,500 in her 100 shares of *Y*'s stock, and *B* had a basis of $3,000 in the promissory note.

In Year One, *Y* had deductible expenses of $32,000, and *Y* had income of $10,000. *Y* made no distributions to *B* in that year. At the end of Year One, the $10,000 of *Y*'s income is allocated to *B* and increases her basis in her *Y* stock to $18,500. The $32,000 of deductible expenses also is allocated to *B*, and the question is how much of that $32,000 can *B* deduct on her individual return for Year One? Since, after making the upward adjustment for B's share of *Y*'s income, B's aggregate basis in *Y*'s stock and debt was $21,500, *B* is limited to a deduction of that amount ($21,500) for that year. For characterization purposes, the $21,500 that *B* can deduct is allocated proportionately among the $32,000 of *Y*'s deductible items. The remaining $10,500 of the deductible expenses that are allocated to *B* is carried over and treated as a deduction incurred by *Y* with respect to *B* in Year Two. The carryover deductions have the same character as they would have had if *B* could have deducted them in Year One. The $10,500 carryover is sometimes referred to as a carryover § 1366(d) loss. *B*'s bases in her stock and her promissory note are reduced to zero.

Ex. (2)   The same facts as those stated in **Ex. (1)**. In Year Two, before taking into account the carryover § 1366(d) loss from Year One, *Y* had income of $2,500, no deductions; and *Y* made no distribution to its shareholder in that year. The $2,500 of *Y*'s income passes through to *B* and increases *B*'s basis in her promissory note. With respect to *B*, *Y* also has a $10,500 carryover § 1366(d) loss that is carried over from Year One; and that loss is treated as incurred by *Y* in Year Two. Only $2,500 of *Y*'s carryover § 1366(d) loss can be deducted by *B* since that is the amount of *B*'s basis in her promissory note after making the adjustment for the income that passed through to *B*. To determine the character of *B*'s deduction, the $2,500 that can be deducted by *B* is allocated proportionately among the $10,500 of deductible items if some of those items have a different character than others.

Y's unused carryover loss of $8,000 will carry over and be treated, with respect to *B*, as a loss incurred by *Y* in the following year (Year Three). At the beginning of Year Three, *B* has a zero basis in both the *Y* stock and debt; and *B* has the potential to qualify to deduct the $8,000 carryover § 1366(d) loss if *B* acquires basis in *Y*'s stock or debt.

In January of Year Three, *B* made a gift to *D* of 40 shares of her *Y* stock. *D* was neither a spouse nor a former spouse of *B*. The $8,000 loss carryover will continue to be potentially available to *B*, and none of it is available to *D*. If, instead, *B* made a gift of all 100 shares of her *Y* stock to *D*, the $8,000 loss carryover would not be available to anyone—in effect, it would cease to exist.

Ex. (3)   The same facts as those stated in **Ex. (2)** except that in Year Two, *Y* had income of $6,000 and deductions of $3,500. The $6,000 of income passes through to *B* first and increases *B*'s basis in her promissory note to $3,000, and increases *B*'s basis in her *Y* stock to $3,000. *Y*'s total deductions for year Two are $14,000 ($10,500 carryover and $3,500 current). Those deductions pass through to *B*, who is limited to a deduction of $6,000 since that is her total basis in her *Y* stock and promissory note after adjusting for her share of the corporation's income. The $6,000 that is deductible by *B* is apportioned among all of the $14,000 of deductible items proportionately to their amounts. Treas. Reg. § 1.1366–2(a)(4). The remaining $8,000 of unused deductions is carried over to the next year (Year Three) with the same character and treated as a deduction incurred by *Y* in that year with respect to *B*. Note that the requirement that the $6,000 that *B* is permitted to deduct be allocated among the $14,000 of *Y*'s deductible items is significant only if some of those deductible items are of a different character than others. At the beginning of Year Three, *B* has a zero basis in both the *Y* stock and note.

§ 2.   Post–Termination Transition Period (PTTP)

If a corporation ceased to be an S corporation at a time when the corporation had § 1366(d) disallowed deductions carried forward with respect to one or more of its shareholders, unless some relief were afforded, the shareholders would lose their potential to obtain use of those deductions. Once the corporation became a C corporation, it could not pass through to its shareholders any of its deductions. In response to that problem, the Code provides a grace period during which such a shareholder can deduct his share of the corporation's carryover § 1366(d) loss to the extent that the shareholder obtains a basis in the stock of the corporation during that period. §§ 1366(d)(3), 1377(b).

In effect, each shareholder is given a period of time in which to increase his basis in the corporation's stock and thereby qualify to deduct that amount of his share of the carryover § 1366(d) loss. Note that only an increase in the basis of stock will permit the deduction of the carryover loss; an increase in the basis of a debt of the corporation during that grace period will not enable the shareholder to deduct any of the carryover loss.

The grace period during which a shareholder can qualify to deduct a carried over loss is called the "post-termination transition period" or "PTTP." The PTTP also serves as a period during which certain distributions can be made from the corporation to a shareholder without causing dividend income to the shareholder even though the corporation has earnings and profits. See Section 2(a) of Chapter 6, infra.

As we shall see, there can be more than one PTTP for a corporation that ceases to be an S corporation. Indeed, it is possible for there to be as many as three separate post-termination transition periods for a corporation. However, one of those three PTTP periods does not apply to the carryover § 1366(d) loss provision.

The deduction of a carryover § 1366(d) loss is permitted only to the extent of the shareholder's basis in the corporation's stock at the close of the last day of *any* post-termination transition period, and the shareholder's basis is reduced by the amount so allowed as a deduction. § 1366(d)(3). However, as described below, one of the three post-termination transition periods does not apply to the carryover § 1366(d) loss provision. Note that the shareholder's basis in the corporation's debt to him will not qualify the shareholder to deduct any part of a carryover § 1366(d) loss in a post-termination transition period.

The post-termination transition period is:

(A) the period beginning on the day after the last day on which the corporation was an S corporation and ending on the later of:

   (1) one year after such last day as an S corporation, or

   (2) the due date for filing a return for the corporation's last taxable year as an S corporation (including extensions), plus

(B) the 120–day period beginning on the date of a *determination* that the corporation's Subchapter S election had terminated for a previous taxable year, plus

(C) the 120–day period beginning on the date of any *determination* pursuant to an audit of the shareholder (after the termination of the S corporation's election) which adjusts a Subchapter S item of income, loss or deduction of the corporation for the most recent continuous period during which it qualified as an S corporation. This third of the three post-termination transition periods does not apply to § 1366(d) carryover losses. § 1377(b)(3)(A).

For purposes of the PTTP provision, a "determination" means any of the following: a court decision that becomes final, a closing agreement made under § 7121, a final disposition by the Service of a claim for refund, an agreement signed by the Secretary and any person relating to that person's tax liability, or an agreement between the corporation and the Service that the corporation failed to qualify as an S corporation. § 1377(b)(2).

Thus, there can be as many as three post-termination transition periods for a corporation whose S election has terminated—one is the one-year period commencing with the first day on which the corporation was a C corporation, a possible second period is the 120–day period that begins with the date on which a determination was made that the corporation's S status had previously terminated, and a possible third period is the 120–day period that begins with the date on which a determination was made adjusting an item of income, deduction of loss of the corporation for the most recent continuous period during which it qualified as an S corporation. However, the third of those three PTTP periods does not apply to the provision allowing a deduction of carryover § 1366(d) losses.

Ex. (1)   As of January 1, Year One, Y Corporation was an S corporation that reports its income on a calendar year basis. *B* owned all 100 shares of Y's outstanding stock, and B had a basis of $10,000 in those shares. In Year One, Y had a net loss of $18,000 which passed through to *B*. Since *B*'s basis in the *Y* stock was only $10,000, *B* was permitted to deduct only that amount of the pass-thru loss. The remaining $8,000 of Y's loss is carried over as a carryover § 1366(d) loss. B's basis in the Y stock was reduced to zero. Y had no net income or loss in Year Two, and so B's basis in the Y stock was still zero at the end of Year Two. The corporation had an $8,000 carryover § 1366(d) loss at the beginning of Year Three. Beginning with January 1, Year Three, *Y* ceased to be an S corporation and became a C corporation. A post-termination transition period therefore began on that date. In Year Three, *Y* earned net income of $18,000. *Y* made no distributions to its shareholder in that year, but on November 6, Year Three, *B* contributed $5,000 cash to *Y* as a contribution to the corporation's capital. Neither of the two 120–day periods that provide additional post-termination transition periods was triggered in this case. The income earned by *Y* in Year Three does not pass through to *B* nor does it affect *B*'s basis in her stock since *Y* was not an S corporation in that year. However, *B*'s contribution to *Y*'s capital will increase her basis in her 100 shares of *Y*'s stock by that amount; and so *B* had a basis of $5,000 in those shares after she made the contribution.

Under § 1366(d)(3), the $8,000 § 1366(d) loss that is carried over from Year Two is treated as having been incurred by *B* on December 31, Year Three (the last day of that post-termination transition period). Since *B* had a basis of $5,000 in her *Y* stock at that date, *B* is permitted to deduct $5,000 of the carryover loss. The remaining $3,000 of the carryover loss can never be deducted. *B*'s basis in her 100 shares of *Y*'s stock is reduced to zero.

The third PTTP, which is described above, is the 120–day period beginning on the day that a determination is made pursuant to an audit that a tax item of the corporation during its last continuous period as an S corporation had to be adjusted. If the adjustment increases the S corporation's income for that year, the portion of that adjustment that is attributable to the shareholder will pass through to the shareholder and thereby increase the shareholder's basis in the corporation's stock as of the close of the year for which the adjustment is made. The problem was that if the corporation, which has become a C corporation, has earnings and profits, how could it distribute the shareholder's portion of the income to the shareholder without causing the shareholder to be taxed on it and thereby be taxed twice on the same income? The 120–day window was adopted by Congress in 1996 to permit a corporation in that position to make a distribution to the shareholder during that 120–day period without causing the shareholder to recognize income. See Sections 2 and 2(a) of Chapter 6, infra, discussing the "Accumulated Adjustments Account" concept.

However, if left unchecked, a shareholder could take advantage of that window by purchasing stock of the corporation during that 120–day period and thereby increase his basis in his stock and qualify an additional amount of carryover § 1366(d) loss for a deduction. In 2004, Congress prevented that from occurring by adding § 1377(b)(3)(A) to the Code, which states that the 120–day window for adjustments does not permit the deduction of a carryover § 1366(d) loss.

This amendment, however, does not prevent the shareholder from deducting an additional amount of the carryover § 1366(d) loss in the year for which the adjustment is made to the S corporation's income. The shareholder will, of course, take into income her share of the income that was added to the corporation by the adjustment, but that additional income will be offset by the deduction of the carryover § 1366(d) loss allowed to the shareholder for the taxable year for which the corporation's income was adjusted because of the increased basis in her stock. Obviously, the deduction cannot exceed the amount of additional income that passed through to the shareholder for that year. The ordinary operation of the tax law allows the shareholder to deduct the carryover loss to the extent of the income that passes through to the shareholder for that earlier year, and thus the shareholder has no need to rely on a special PTTP in order to utilize any amount of the loss to the extent that the shareholder held stock of the S corporation in that earlier year. In that light, the 2004 amendment served to make that special PTTP inapplicable to the § 1366(d) carryover loss provision. The treatment of distributions from the corporation to the shareholder during that 120–day period is discussed in Section 2(a) of Chapter 6, infra.

Ex. (2) The same facts as those stated in **Ex. (1)** except that *B* did not contribute any money or property to *Y* in Year Three. Therefore, none of *X*'s $8,000 of carryover § 1366(d) loss can be deducted by *B* at the end of that year, which is the end of the PTTP. On April 1, Year Five, pursuant to an audit, the IRS determined that the income reported by *Y* for Year Two was understated and that *Y*'s income was $6,000 greater than reported. Assume that that determination by IRS qualified as a "determination" for the purposes of § 1377(b)(2). As a result of that determination, *B*'s income for Year Two was increased by $6,000. *B*'s basis in her *Y* stock was increased from zero to $6,000.

Thus, at the end of Year Two, *B* had $6,000 of pass-thru income from *Y*. But, *B* also had $6,000 of basis in her *Y* stock because of having that pass-thru income. Since *B* had $6,000 of stock basis at the end of Year Two, she is permitted to deduct $6,000 of the corporation's $8,000 of carryover § 1366(d) loss in that year. Unless the character of that loss deduction differs from the character of the income, it will offset the $6,000 of income that *B* recognized in Year Two. In effect, *B*'s income and deduction would be a wash, and *B* would not incur any net income from the adjustments made because of the IRS's determination. Therefore, the denial of the use of the PTTP to allow a shareholder to deduct a carryover § 1366(d) loss does not cause any undue hardship. As of the beginning of Year Three, *Y* will have a carryover $2,000 § 1366(d) loss; and *B* will have a zero basis in her stock.

Ex. (3)   The same facts as those stated in **Ex. (2)** except that on May 4, Year Five, *B* purchased additional Y stock for $4,000 and thereby increased her aggregate basis in her *Y* stock from zero to $4,000. Section 1366(d)(3)(A) provides that a loss deduction that was denied for the last year in which a corporation was an S corporation is treated as incurred by a shareholder on the last day of "any" post-termination transition period. If that provision were applicable, *B* would be deemed to have incurred the corporation's carryover loss on July 29, Year Five, when the 120–day period following the IRS determination expired. Since *B* had $4,000 of basis in her stock at that time, she would be permitted to deduct the $2,000 carryover § 1366(d) loss. To prevent that from occurring, Congress added § 1377(b)(3)(A) which provides that the PTTP provision for the 120–day period following a determination adjusting the income of an S corporation does not apply to carryover § 1366(d) losses. Consequently, *B* cannot deduct any of the $2,000 carryover loss.

§ 3.   Worthless Securities and Non-business Bad Debts

If a shareholder's stock or debt of an S corporation becomes worthless, the deduction and loss items of the corporation that pass through to the shareholder in that taxable year will be deducted by the shareholder and reduce the shareholder's basis in the corporation's stock and debt instruments before a deduction is taken under § 165(g) for worthless securities or under § 166(d) for nonbusiness bad debts. § 1367(b)(3).

§ 4. At Risk and Passive Activity Loss Limitations

In addition to the limitations imposed by § 1366(d) on the deductibility of a shareholder's share of an S corporation's losses and deductions, a shareholder is also subject to the "at risk" limitations of § 465 and the passive activity loss and credit limitations of § 469. The at risk limitations and the passive activity loss and credit limitations are not applied to the S corporation itself. §§ 465(a)(1); 469(a)(2); Temp. Reg. § 1.469–1T(b), (g)(2). Since the tax items of an S corporation are passed through to its shareholders, who themselves are subject to the at risk and passive activity loss and credit limitations, there is no reason to subject an S corporation to those limitations.

There is an order of priority to the application of these limitations to a shareholder's share of an S corporation's deductions and losses. First, the limitation imposed by § 1366(d) is applied. Any amount that is deductible after applying § 1366(d) is then subjected to the at risk limitation of § 465. Finally, any amount of deduction that is not precluded by §§ 1366(d) and 465 is subjected to the limitations imposed on passive activity losses by § 469. See Temp. Reg. § 1.469–2T(d)(6). The manner in which such disallowed losses are allocated among the shareholder's share of the corporation's losses is described in Temp. Reg. § 1.469–2T(d)(6). Note that corporate losses that are allocated to a shareholder and that are deductible under § 1366(d) will reduce the shareholder's basis in his stock or corporate debt regardless of whether the shareholder is prevented from deducting the loss by the at risk or passive activity loss rules.

The at risk limitation is applied separately to each activity from which a taxpayer has income. § 465(c). In special circumstances, the tax items of certain activities can be aggregated for this purpose so that the losses from one such activity can offset the income from another without regard to the amount that the taxpayer has at risk. A loss that is disallowed by the at risk limitation can be carried forward and deducted in a subsequent year when the at risk rule is satisfied, provided that the deduction is not then denied by the passive activity loss limitation of § 469. § 465(a)(2).

If an S corporation has losses from one activity and a gain from a different activity, must the corporation's shareholders segregate their share of the items from each activity before applying the at risk rules? When an S corporation is engaged in more than one trade or business, such trades or businesses can be combined and treated as a single activity if at least 65 percent of the corporation's losses for the taxable year in question are allocated to shareholders who actively participate in the management of the corporation's trades or businesses. § 465(c)(3)(B). This aggregation provision does not apply to portfolio investment; it applies only to trades or businesses.

Unlike the at risk rules, the limitation on the deduction of passive activity losses does not operate on each activity separately. Instead, the tax items from all passive activities are aggregated and the limitation is applied to the net loss (if any). § 469(d)(1). An activity of an S corporation is passive as to a shareholder if it involves the conduct of a trade or business in which the shareholder does not materially participate. § 469(c)(1). It is necessary to determine separately for each activity of the S corporation whether the shareholder's participation is material. Temp. Reg. § 1.469–2T(e)(1). A loss that is disallowed by the passive activity loss limitation rule can be carried forward and deducted in a subsequent year in which that rule is satisfied. § 469(b).

An activity which does not constitute a trade or business will not be treated as a passive activity. For example, a portfolio investment is not a passive activity. However, apart from portfolio investments, many profit-oriented activities that do not constitute a trade or business for purposes of § 162 (the business expense deduction provision) nevertheless will be treated as a trade or business for purposes of the passive activity loss limitation provision. § 469(c)(5), (6).

Even though the passive activity loss rules operate on the S corporation's activities in the aggregate, if the corporation has more than one activity, it will still be necessary to keep track of each activity separately. There are several reasons why this is so. There may be losses from an activity that are being carried over under § 469(b) because a deduction was denied by § 469(a). Such losses can be deducted when the corporation's entire interest in that activity is terminated. § 469(g). So, it is necessary to know the amount of carryover losses that is attributable to a discontinued activity. Also, as noted above, the shareholder's participation in each activity must be measured annually to determine whether that activity is a passive activity within the meaning of § 469.

A taxpayer materially participates in a trade or business if the taxpayer and his spouse are involved in the operation of that trade or business on a basis that is "regular, continuous and substantial." § 469(h)(1), (5). So, the applicability of the passive activity loss limitations to a shareholder's portion of an S corporation's loss from a trade or business depends upon the extent and type of the participation in the conduct of that trade or business by the shareholder and his spouse. If the shareholder and his spouse materially participate in the conduct of a trade or business, the shareholder's share of losses from that activity will not constitute passive activity losses.

Treasury has promulgated extensive regulations concerning the passive activity loss and credit rules. A temporary regulation establishes seven tests for determining whether there has been material participation in a trade or business, and those seven tests are exclusive. Temp. Reg. § 1.469–5T(a). Satisfaction of any one of the seven tests is sufficient to establish material participation.

Certain designated activities are included in or excluded from the passive activity loss limitation provision by statutory fiat without regard to whether the activity is a trade or business in which the taxpayer materially participates. For example, subject to limited exceptions in the statute and regulations, rental activity is treated as a passive activity for purposes of this provision. § 469(c)(2), (7).

§ 5. Other Limitations

The Code imposes a number of limitations on the availability of certain deductions and credits. For S corporations, in many cases, these limitations will be applied at the shareholder level rather than at the corporate level. This is so, for example, for the at risk limitation, the passive activity loss and credit limitation, and for the limitation on the amount of charitable contributions that can be deducted. However, there are limitations that are applied both at the entity level and at the shareholder level as well. For example, the dollar limitation on the amount of cost of certain depreciable items that can be expensed under § 179 in a taxable year is determined first at the entity level as to the S corporation itself. A portion of such expense allowed to the S corporation by § 179(b) is allocated to each shareholder and that allocated amount is then added to the other such expenses that the shareholder had in that year. The combined total is subjected to the § 179(b) dollar limitation. § 179(d)(8).

CHAPTER 6

DISTRIBUTIONS RECEIVED FROM AN S CORPORATION

§ 1. In General

Distributions of cash or other property made from an S corporation to a shareholder will not be treated as a dividend if the corporation has no *e and p*. § 1368(a), (b). As previously noted, an S corporation can have *e and p* only if it accumulated *e and p* in a prior year in which it was a C corporation, or if it inherited the *e and p* of another corporation pursuant to a reorganization or liquidation. If the corporation has no *e and p*, the amount of the distribution will reduce the shareholder's basis in his stock (but not in his debt instruments) and any excess of the distribution over the stock's basis is treated as a gain from the sale of the stock. § 1368(b).

§ 2. Accumulated Adjustments Account (AAA)

If an S corporation has accumulated *e and p*, the portion of the distributions that it makes to its shareholders in a taxable year that is not in excess of the corporation's "accumulated adjustments account" is treated the same as if that portion were distributed by a corporation that had no *e and p*—i.e., it reduces a distributee's basis in his stock, and any excess over his basis in his stock is treated as gain from the sale of that stock. § 1368(c)(1). The accumulated adjustments account provision applies to distributions of cash, property in kind, or both. The portion of the corporation's distributions that are in excess of its accumulated adjustments account are treated as dividends to the extent of the corporation's *e and p*.

An S corporation's accumulated adjustments account is an account for the corporation itself; the shareholders do not have an account in their individual capacity. Consequently, in a taxable year when an S corporation with earnings and profits makes a single distribution to a single shareholder, the entire accumulated adjustments account of the corporation is applicable to that distribution, as contrasted to making only a fractional share (determined by the percentage of stock held by the shareholder) of the accumulated adjustments account available. The accumulated adjustments account is not apportioned among the shareholders. Treas. Reg. § 1.1368–2(a). However, unless the corporation's taxable year is divided into several parts under one of two special provisions, if distributions are made to more than one shareholder during the corporation's taxable year in a total amount that exceeds the accumulated adjustments account, then the accumulated adjustments account, as determined at the close of the taxable year, is apportioned among the distributions in proportion to their amounts. § 1368(c) (flush line).

The corporation's "accumulated adjustments account," which term is defined in § 1368(e)(1), is an account of the aggregate amount of most of the adjustments made under § 1367 to the basis that shareholders have in their shares of stock and debt instruments of the corporation because of the allocation to the shareholders of tax items of the corporation. The accumulated adjustment account is sometimes referred to as the "AAA." For taxable years beginning after August 17, 1998, the order in which the several adjustments to AAA are made is set forth in Treas. Reg. § 1.1368–2(a)(5). As noted above, it is the S corporation's account; the shareholders do not have their own accounts, nor is the account apportioned among them according to their stock holdings.

An accumulated adjustment account will ordinarily not need to be maintained for a corporation that has always been an S corporation, unless it is a successor to a C corporation as a result of a reorganization or liquidation transaction, because such an S corporation will not have any accumulated *e and p*. Even with respect to an S corporation that previously had accumulated *e and p* as a result of having previously been a C corporation or being a successor to a C corporation, the S corporation will not need to maintain an AAA if it has previously distributed all of its accumulated *e & p* to its shareholders.

On the first day that a corporation is an S corporation, its AAA is zero. Its AAA is then increased or decreased by the adjustments required by § 1368(e)(1). Only adjustments attributable to the most recent continuous period that the corporation was an S corporation are taken into account, and no adjustments for a taxable year beginning prior to 1983 are taken into account. § 1368(e)(1)(A), (2). In certain circumstances, transitional rules apply for distributions of income that was earned in pre–1983 years. See Section 4 of this chapter. The most recent continuous period, including only taxable years that began after 1982, that a corporation has been an S corporation is referred to as the "S period." § 1368(e)(2). Thus, except for the application of the post-termination transition period rules, which are discussed in Section 2(a) of this chapter, once a corporation's status as an S corporation is terminated, its then existing AAA ceases to be of any use even if the corporation subsequently makes a new election for Subchapter S treatment in a later year. However, if a termination is inadvertent, the shareholders may qualify for special relief under § 1362(f). See Section 4 of Chapter 7, infra.

As noted above, the adjustments made to the AAA are similar to those made to the shareholder's basis in stock or debt by § 1377, but there are a few differences. One difference is that no adjustment will be made to the AAA for tax-exempt income and expenses related to that income. Consequently, tax-exempt income will not increase the corporation's AAA, and the expenses connected with that income will not reduce the corporation's AAA. Another difference is that the corporation's AAA can be reduced below zero so as to become a negative figure. Also, no adjustment is made for federal taxes paid or accrued by the S corporation that are attributable to a period when the corporation was a C corporation. § 1368(e)(1)(A).

Since losses incurred by an S corporation will reduce its shareholders' bases in the stock and debt instruments of the corporation that they hold, such losses also will reduce the corporation's AAA. However, another difference from § 1377 adjustments is that losses or deductions that are not deductible by a shareholder because of insufficiency of basis in the corporation's stock or debt nevertheless will reduce the corporation's AAA. Of course, if the shareholder subsequently is allowed to deduct the item because of having acquired basis in a later year, which deduction will reduce the shareholder's newly acquired basis, no additional adjustment is made to the AAA. Treas. Reg. § 1.1368–2(a)(3)(ii).

An S corporation's AAA is reduced for distributions made to its shareholders that are not made out of its *e and p* even if that distribution resulted in gain to a shareholder, but a distribution cannot cause or increase the amount of a negative AAA.

Section 1368(e)(1)(A) provides that the accumulated adjustments account can be reduced below zero, and so it is possible for a corporation to have a negative AAA. If that occurs, the corporation will not have a useful accumulated adjustments account until its subsequent net positive adjustments exceed that negative figure.

A "net negative adjustment" is the excess of reductions in the AAA for a taxable year (other than reductions for corporate distributions) over increases in the AAA for such year. If there is a "net negative adjustment" to the corporation's AAA for a taxable year, the amount of AAA at the end of the year that is to be applied to distributions made during that year is determined without making any adjustment for the "net negative adjustment." § 1368(e)(1)(C) In other words, the "negative adjustment" for a taxable year is not taken into account when determining the AAA to be applied to corporate distributions made during that year.

In the event that some shares of an S corporation's stock are redeemed in a transaction that is treated as a purchase under § 302(a) or § 303, the corporation's AAA is reduced by an amount that bears the same ratio to the AAA as the number of redeemed shares bears to the total number of shares that were outstanding immediately prior to the redemption. § 1368(e)(1)(B). If a corporation has a negative accumulated adjustments account, a § 302(a) or § 303 redemption of some of the corporation's stock will reduce the negative balance of the AAA in the same manner as it would reduce a positive balance. Treas. Reg. § 1.1368–2(d)(1). If a distribution that a shareholder receives in a redemption of stock is treated as a § 301 distribution (rather than as a purchase), it will be protected from dividend treatment by any available AAA and will reduce the amount of the AAA accordingly.

In the event that an S corporation makes both ordinary and redemption distributions in the same taxable year, the AAA is adjusted first for any ordinary distributions and then for any redemption distributions. The significance of providing that order of priority is that the AAA can insulate a shareholder from income for ordinary distributions before reducing the AAA because of redemptions. A "redemption distribution" does not include redemptions to the extent they are treated as § 301 distributions. Id.

Adjustments that are made to a corporation's AAA are independent of adjustments to be made to its *e and p*. The normal rules for adjusting *e and p* are applied to an S corporation's *e and p* for dividend distributions, redemptions, liquidations, reorganizations and divisions. Id. An S corporation's *e and p* are not adjusted for income or deductions arising while it is an S corporation.

If an S corporation acquires the assets of another S corporation pursuant to a reorganization or the liquidation of a controlled subsidiary (i.e., in a transaction to which § 381(a) applies), the AAA of the two corporations (whether positive or negative) will be merged. Treas. Reg. § 1.1368–2(d)(2). In the case of certain (but not all) corporate divisions to which § 355 or § 356 applies, the AAA of the distributing corporation will be allocated between the distributing and the controlled corporations. Treas. Reg. § 1.1368–2(d)(3).

In general, the purpose of the AAA is to permit an S corporation to make nondividend distributions to its shareholders in an amount equal to its net post–1982 income that was previously taxed to its shareholders. The availability of this provision to a distributee does not depend upon the distributee's having been a shareholder at the time that the corporation earned the income that constitutes the AAA. A distribution to a shareholder can be insulated from dividend treatment by the AAA provision even though that shareholder had not previously been taxed on any of the corporation's income because, for example, the shareholder had only recently acquired stock of the corporation. The amount of AAA that is available for corporate distributions typically is determined at the end of the taxable year. As discussed later in this section, there are circumstances in which an S corporation's taxable year can be divided into two parts, each of which is treated as a separate year.

If all of the shareholders who received a distribution from the corporation during a taxable year consent, the corporation can waive the accumulated adjustments account provision as to all the distributions made in that year § 1368(e)(3). This election eliminates the AAA provision for the taxable year for which the election is effective. If this election is made, the corporation's distributions will constitute dividends to the extent of the corporation's accumulated *e and p*. One reason for making this election is to reduce accumulated *e and p* to zero and thereby preclude a tax on passive investment income under § 1375 and to preclude a termination of the Subchapter S election under § 1362(d)(3). See Chapter 8 and Section 7 of Chapter 7.

The amount of the distributions to shareholders that is treated as a dividend (i.e., the amount of such distributions that is not insulated from dividend treatment by an accumulated adjustments account or by some other provision and that does not exceed the corporation's accumulated *e and p*) will reduce the corporation's *e and p*.

If a corporation with both accumulated *e and p* and an AAA makes more than one distribution during a taxable year and if the aggregate of such distributions is greater than its accumulated adjustments account at the end of the year, it is necessary to determine the manner in which the AAA is to be allocated among the several distributions. Section 1368(c) provides that, in such cases, the AAA is to be determined at the end of the taxable year and allocated among the distributions in proportion to their respective amounts.

Congress wished Treasury to provide relief from the pro rata allocation rule when there is a substantial change in the proportional holding of the corporation's stock during the taxable year in which the distributions were made. The regulations accommodate that purpose by permitting an S corporation to elect to divide its taxable year into two separate taxable years when there has been a "qualifying disposition" of its stock. The first of these two short taxable years ends on the day in which the qualifying disposition occurs. Treas. Reg. § 1.1368–1(g)(2). If that election is made, each of the two short years is treated as a separate taxable year. As a result, all of the corporation's tax items for that year (including adjustments to *e and p,* basis, and AAA) must be apportioned between the two years; and the treatment of distributions made in each short year must be determined separately.

A "qualifying disposition" occurs when one of the following three events takes place during a 30–day period within the corporation's taxable year:

(1) a shareholder disposes of 20% or more of the corporation's outstanding stock;

(2) 20% or more of the corporation's outstanding stock is redeemed from one shareholder under § 302(a) or § 303; or

(3) stock equal to or greater than 25% of the corporation's previously outstanding stock is issued to one or more new shareholders.

If a disposition of stock is taken into account in determining whether there was a qualifying disposition, another disposition of that same stock will not be taken into account to determine whether a subsequent qualifying disposition occurred. Treas. Reg. § 1.1368–1(g)(2).

If the events that caused a qualifying disposition also caused the termination of a shareholder's entire interest so that an election to divide the taxable year can be made under § 1377(a)(2), the latter section has priority; and an election cannot then be made under Treas. Reg. § 1.1368–1(g)(2). The only election that is available in that case is the one provided by § 1377(a)(2). That election is discussed at Section 6 of Chapter 7, infra. See Treas. Reg. §§ 1.1368–1(g)(2)(iv), 1.1377–1(b)(1).

(a) Distributions Made During Post–Termination Transition Period

A distribution of *cash* from a corporation to a shareholder after the termination of the corporation's Subchapter S status, but during a PTTP (i.e., a post-termination transition period, the three periods of which are described in Section 2 of Chapter 5, supra) will not be taxed as a dividend to the shareholder to the extent that the distribution does not exceed the corporation's accumulated adjustments account (AAA), but instead such cash distributions will be applied against and reduce the shareholder's basis in his stock. § 1371(e)(1). This provision applies only to distributions to persons who were shareholders of the corporation at the time that its S corporation status was terminated. Treas. Reg. § 1.1377–2(b). Moreover, it appears that the amount excluded from dividend treatment by this provision cannot exceed the shareholder's basis in the corporation's stock since the provision requires that the distribution reduce the shareholder's basis in his stock. Note that only cash distributions qualify for this treatment, and the exclusion from dividend treatment applies even if the distributing corporation has *e and p*.

If the total amount of distributions during a PTTP exceeds the corporation's AAA, the AAA will be allocated among the distributions in proportion to the amount of each distribution. However, in making that allocation, presumably distributions to which the AAA provision does not apply are disregarded. For example, since the AAA provision does not apply to a distribution during a PTTP to a person who was not a shareholder at the time that the corporation's status as an S corporation was terminated, distributions to such persons should be disregarded in making the allocation of the AAA.

This provision permits a corporation with accumulated or current *e and p* to make a nondividend distribution of earnings that it accumulated while it was an S corporation even though its Subchapter S status has been terminated, provided that it makes the distribution within one of three specified periods after the termination occurred. Only AAA that was acquired during the corporation's S period can be utilized. § 1368(e)(1)(A). The "S period" is the most recent continuous period (excluding any year beginning prior to 1983) during which the corporation was an S corporation. § 1368(e)(2).

However, as to one of the three post-termination transition periods,—i.e., the 120–day period following a determination, pursuant to an audit, that made an adjustment to one or more tax items of the corporation that were incurred during its S period—the AAA is computed differently than it is for the other two post-termination transition periods. For that 120–day period, the AAA consists only of the net positive adjustment made to the AAA because of the modifications required by the determination that was made pursuant to the audit. § 1377(b)(3)(B).

If all the shareholders to whom distributions were made during a post-termination transition period consent, the corporation can waive the AAA provision as to all distributions made during that period. § 1371(e)(2). If that election is made, distributions will be treated as made first out of the corporation's earnings and profits and so will be dividend income to the shareholders. The reason that parties might make this election is to avoid the imposition of accumulated earnings or personal holding surtaxes on the corporation. See §§ 535(a), 545(a), and 561.

Ex. (1)   As of December 31 of Year Five, *X* Corporation, which reports on a calendar year basis, had been an S corporation for three years and had been a C corporation for two years prior to that period. *X* had two equal shareholders, individuals *A* and *B*. At the end of Year Five, *X* had an accumulated adjustments account (AAA) of $18,000; and *X* had accumulated earnings and profits of $15,000 which it had accumulated in a prior period when it had been a C corporation. *A* and *B* had a zero basis in their stock, and *X* owed no debts to either shareholder. *X* had no carryover § 1366(d) losses.

On January 1, Year Six, *X* ceased to be an S corporation and therefore became a C corporation. In Year Six, *X* had current earnings and profits of $4,000. On September 8, Year Six, *X* distributed $5,000 cash to each of its shareholders; and *X* made no other distributions that year. The corporation did not elect to preclude the application of the PTTP provision under § 1371(e)(2). Nevertheless, the distribution is dividend income to each shareholder—i.e., $2,000 of each distribution is made out of current *e and p*, and the remaining $3,000 is made out of accumulated *e and p*. Since *X* no longer is an S corporation, § 1368(c), dealing with distributions from an S corporation with an AAA, does not apply. Also, the PTTP provision of § 1371(e)(1) does not seem to apply since the shareholders had no basis in their stock; and it appears that that provision applies only to the extent that the distribution reduces the shareholder's basis in stock. As a result, the distributions are not insulated from dividend treatment. *X*'s accumulated *e and p* is reduced by $10,000.

Ex. (2)   The same facts as those stated in **Ex. (1)** except that on August 19, Year Six, *A* purchased additional shares of stock from X for $4,000. When the distribution was made to the shareholders on September 8, *X* distributed $4,000 cash to *B* and $6,000 cash to A. When the $6,000 distribution was made to A in September, A had a basis of $4,000 in his X stock. Since A received the distribution during a post-termination transition period and the corporation had an adequate amount of AAA, $4,000 of the amount that A received reduces his basis in his stock to zero; and the remaining $2,000 of the distribution is dividend income to A. As discussed in **Ex. (1)**, all of the $4,000 distributed to B is dividend income. X's AAA is reduced by $4,000 and its accumulated *e and p* is reduced by $6,000.

Ex. (3)   The same facts as those stated in **Ex. (2)** except that on February 11, Year Six, A sold all of his X stock to D, an individual for $10,000. On August 19, D purchased additional shares of stock from X for $4,000. On September 8, X distributed $6,000 cash to D and $4,000 cash to B. X made no other distributions that year. Since D was not a shareholder of X on the date of the termination of its status as an S corporation, the PTTP rules do not apply to the distribution to D. Therefore, all of the distributions to the two shareholders are dividend income to them.

Ex. (4)   The same facts as those stated in **Ex. (1)** except that no distribution was made to the shareholders in Years Six or Seven. Early in Year Eight, the IRS began auditing B's tax return for Year Six. On

June 5, Year Eight, under § 7121, the IRS executed a closing agreement with *A, B,* and *X* that *X*'s gross income in Year Six was $3,000 greater than reported, and that each of the shareholders incurred a tax deficiency for Year Six because of having $1,500 additional pass-thru income from the corporation. The closing agreement constituted a "determination" within the meaning of § 1377(b)(2).

The adjustment to *X*'s Year Six income increased the zero basis of each shareholder's stock to $1,500, and increased *X*'s AAA by $3,000 so that it became $21,000. On July 3 of Year Eight, *A* purchased additional shares of stock from *X* for $4,000. On August 7, Year Eight, *X* distributed $6,000 cash to *A* and $3,000 cash to *B*. On that date, *A* had a basis of $5,500 in his *X* stock, and *B* had a basis of $1,500 in her *X* stock. *X* had *e and p* of over $25,000 at that time. *X* made no other distributions in Year Eight.

The August 7 distribution was within a PTTP since it was within 120 days after the IRS determination that added $3,000 to *X*'s income for Year Six. To the extent that a distribution to a shareholder does not exceed the lesser of the corporation's AAA or the shareholder's basis in his stock, it will merely reduce the shareholder's basis. Since the distribution was made during the PTTP for the 120–day period following a determination of an adjustment to the corporation's income, the AAA is limited to the aggregate additions to it that was made as a consequence of the modification caused by that determination.

Thus, for purposes of measuring the amount of dividend income from the August, Year Eight distributions, the AAA of the corporation is only $3,000. Since the total amount distributed ($9,000) is greater than the $3,000 AAA, the AAA must be apportioned between the two distributions according to their respective amounts. So, 2/3 of the $3,000 of AAA (i.e., $2,000) is allocated to the distribution made to A. Of the $6,000 distributed to A in August, Year Eight, $2,000 reduces his basis in his stock from $5,500 to $3,500; and the remaining $4,000 of the distribution he received is dividend income. X had ample *e and p* to classify as a dividend the portion of the distribution that was not insulated by the PTTP provision.

Of the $3,000 that was distributed to B in August, Year Eight, 1/3 of the $3,000 of AAA is allocated to that distribution. B reduces her $1,500 basis in her stock by $1,000 so that she then has a basis of $500 in her stock. The remaining $2,000 of the distribution she received is treated as dividend income.

§ 3. Distribution of Appreciated or Depreciated Property

As is true for C corporations, if an S corporation makes a distribution of appreciated property (other than its own obligation) with respect to its stock, the corporation will recognize gain as if the corporation had sold the property to the distributee at its fair market value. § 311(b). A similar recognition rule applies to liquidating distributions of appreciated property. § 336(a). The S corporation will be taxed on such recognized gains only to the extent that they constitute a "recognized built-in gain" taxed under § 1374 or passive investment income taxed under § 1375. See Chapters 8 and 9.

If an S corporation distributes depreciated property as a nonliquidating distribution, it will not recognize any loss. § 311(a). If an S corporation distributes depreciated property as a liquidating distribution, its loss will be recognized in some circumstances, but not in others. § 336(a), (d). A loss that is recognized will pass through to the shareholders, but a loss that is not recognized will not.

Regardless of whether all or any of the gain from the distribution of appreciated property causes the S corporation to incur a tax liability, the gain that is recognized by the S corporation (effectively reduced by the taxes, if any, incurred by the corporation thereon under

§ 1374 or § 1375) will pass through to its shareholders. § 1366(a), (f)(2), (3). The gain that is passed through to a shareholder will increase that shareholder's basis in the corporation's stock.

The requirement that an S corporation recognize gain on distributing appreciated property generally does not apply to a distribution of certain properties that is made in connection with a corporate reorganization or division that qualifies for §§ 354, 355 or 356 treatment.

Unless the distribution of the appreciated property constitutes a dividend or the shareholder's adjusted basis in his stock (after adjusting his basis for the shareholder's share of the corporation's gain) is less than the amount distributed to him, a shareholder will not recognize income on the receipt of the distribution. Of course, each shareholder will recognize income from the pass through of the S corporation's recognized gain; but the distribution itself usually will not cause a second tax to the shareholders.

§ 4. Distribution of Pre–1983 Accumulated *E and P*

Unless the accumulated adjustments account provision applies, a shareholder of an S corporation can recognize dividend income on receiving a distribution if the corporation has accumulated *e and p*. An S corporation can have *e and p* only if it was accumulated either in a year in which the corporation was a C corporation or if it was inherited pursuant to a corporate reorganization or liquidation. The accumulated adjustments account does not include any income or other tax items that were earned by the S corporation in a taxable year that began prior to 1983. The pre–1983 limitation arises as a consequence of the major changes that were made to Subchapter S by the Subchapter S Revision Act of 1982 (SRA). The question then is how can an S corporation that has accumulated *e and p* distribute to its shareholders its pre–1983 earnings without causing them to have dividend income? That problem arises only when the distribution by the S corporation exceeds its accumulated adjustments account.

Congress addressed that problem in the SRA itself by adopting transitional rules in § 1379, which permit the pre-SRA rules to apply to distributions made from pre–1983 earnings in certain circumstances. Under § 1379(c), in certain circumstances, earnings of an S corporation in years prior to 1983 that were passed through to its shareholders (such earnings are referred to as "previously taxed income") can be distributed under the protection of the pre-SRA tax rules. Those tax rules exclude certain types of cash distributions from dividend treatment. The following three conditions must be satisfied: (1) the S corporation has undistributed previously taxed income from a pre-SRA year in which the corporation was an S corporation; (2) the corporation's election under Subchapter S has remained in continuous effect; and (3) the distribution in the post-SRA year is made in cash. If those requirements are met, the pre-SRA provision for the distribution of previously taxed income applies and the distribution can escape dividend treatment. § 1379(c); Treas. Reg. § 1.1368–1(d)(2).

§ 5. Illustration

Ex. *X* Corporation was formed by unrelated individuals *A*, *B* and *C* in Year One. Each shareholder acquired 30 shares of voting common stock of *X*, and the corporation had no other shares outstanding. *X* and its shareholders report their income on a calendar year basis. As of January 1, Year Three, *X* had accumulated earnings and profits of $60,000, and each shareholder had a basis of $35,000 in the 30 shares of *X*'s stock that he held. Year Three is subsequent to 1982. Effective January 1, Year Three, *X* became an S corporation pursuant to a valid election. In Year Three, *X* had net income of $45,000 which was allocated equally among *A*, *B* and *C*. *X* made no distributions to its shareholders in Year Three. All of the income and deductions that comprised *X*'s $45,000 of net income constituted nonseparately computed income or loss. None of *X*'s income in any of the years mentioned in this example constituted either passive investment income or built-in gain.

The $15,000 of X's net income for Year Three that was allocated to each shareholder is included in that shareholder's income for Year Three and increased that shareholder's basis in his X stock. Accordingly, as of the beginning of Year Four, each shareholder had a basis of $50,000 in his 30 shares of X's stock. Also, as of the beginning of Year Four, X had an accumulated adjustments account (AAA) of $45,000 since that was the aggregate amount by which X's three shareholders increased their bases in their X stock. X's earnings and profits are not affected by the income that it earned as an S corporation. So, as of the beginning of Year Four X continued to have accumulated earnings and profits of $60,000.

In Year Four, X had net income of $24,000, and all of the income and deductions that comprised that net income constituted nonseparately computed income or loss. On October 1, Year Four, A sold his 30 shares of X's stock to F for $72,000 cash. No election was made under either § 1377(a)(2) or Treas. Reg. § 1.1368–1(g)(2) to divide Year Four into two taxable years. On October 31, Year Four, X distributed $40,000 cash to F. On December 31, Year Four, X distributed $40,000 cash to B and $40,000 cash to C. X made no other distributions in Year Four. No election was made under

§ 1368(e)(3) to preclude the application of the accumulated adjustments account provision to any of the distributions.

In Year Four, *B* and *C* each recognized $8,000 of income as their share of *X*'s net income for that year. This amount increased the basis that *B* and *C* each had in his *X* stock. The remaining $8,000 of *X*'s net income for Year Four is allocated $6,000 to *A* and $2,000 to *F* (their share of *X*'s income is allocated on a daily basis, and *A* held his shares for 75 percent of the year and *F* held his shares for 25 percent of the year). The $6,000 of income allocated to *A* increased his basis in his *X* stock to $56,000, and so *A* recognized a gain of $16,000 on the sale of his stock to *F*. The $2,000 of income allocated to *F* increased his basis in his *X* stock to $74,000.

X's accumulated adjustments account, which was $45,000 at the beginning of Year Four, is increased by the $24,000 of adjustments made to the bases of its shareholders' stock as a consequence of the income pass-thru that took place in Year Four. So, by the end of Year Four, before taking into account the effect that the distributions *X* made that year will have on the AAA, *X* had an accumulated adjustments account of $69,000.

The tax consequences to *F*, *B*, and *C* of the distributions that *X* made to them in Year Four turn upon the size of the accumulated adjustments account that *X* had at the end of that year and upon the amount of their basis in their stock. Since the total amount distributed in Year Four ($120,000) is greater than X's accumulated adjustments account, as determined at the end of Year Four, the AAA is allocated pro rata among the distributions made that year according to the amount distributed.

Since the amount distributed to F that year constituted one-third of the total amount of distributions made by X, one-third of X's $69,000 accumulated adjustments account ($23,000) is allocated to that distribution. Thus, of the $40,000 distributed to F, $23,000 is treated as a recovery of F's basis in his 30 shares of X's stock, and so F's basis in those shares is reduced from $74,000 to $51,000. While there is a question whether the entire $2,000 of X's income that is allocated to F should be added to F's stock basis for the purpose of determining whether the nondividend portion of the distribution exceeded his basis, or whether only the portion of that amount that is attributable to the period prior to F's receipt of the distribution, in this case, it does not matter which approach is chosen since F will have more than sufficient basis in either case. The remaining $17,000 of the amount distributed to F is treated as a dividend paid out of X's accumulated earnings and profits. F will then report $17,000 of dividend income and will report no income for his receipt of the $23,000 of the distribution that is treated as a return of his capital. X's earnings and profits of $60,000 is reduced by the $17,000 of the distribution to F that is treated as a dividend. So, X's earnings and profits are reduced to $43,000.

Another one-third of X's $69,000 accumulated adjustments account ($23,000) is allocated to the $40,000 distribution that was made to C (since B is identically situated to C, the distribution to B will have the same tax consequence as the distribution to C has). That $23,000 of the distribution will be income to C only to the extent that it exceeds C's basis in his stock at the time of the distribution. C had a basis of $50,000 in his stock at the beginning of the year. As noted previously, it is likely that C's share of X's income for the entire year will be added to his stock basis before determining the tax consequence of the distribution, but it is possible that only the portion earned prior to the distribution will be taken into account. Since the distribution was made on the last day of the year, the result will be the same in this case regardless of which approach is adopted. In any event, since C's basis at the beginning of the year was considerably greater than the $23,000 of the distribution that is attributable to the corporation's accumulated adjustments account, none of that $23,000 causes C to recognize any income, but C must reduce his basis in his 30 shares of X's stock by that amount. The remaining $17,000 of the amount distributed to *C* is treated as dividend income to *C* and reduces *X*'s accumulated earnings and profits to $26,000. As a consequence of the distribution to *B*, *X*'s accumulated earnings and profits are reduced by another $17,000, and so are reduced to $9,000.

The difference in the timing of *F*'s distribution from those made to *B* and *C* will not cause a second class of stock classification.

As of the beginning of Year Five, *X's* accumulated adjustments account has been reduced to zero. Also, as of that date, *X* has accumulated earnings and profits of $9,000.

In Year Five, *X*'s income and deductions were equal so that it had no net income or loss for that year. On April 12, Year Five, *X* distributed $10,000 cash each to *B*, *C*, and *F*. *X* made no other distributions in that year. As noted above, *X* had exhausted its accumulated adjustments account in Year Four; and since *X* had no net income in Year Five, *X* did not acquire any accumulated adjustments account in that year. Consequently, the entire $10,000 distribution to each shareholder will constitute dividend income to the extent of *X*'s accumulated earnings and profits. So, $3,000 (1/3 of $9,000) of the amount distributed to each shareholder constitutes dividend income. The remaining $7,000 of each distribution is treated as a return of the shareholders' capital and thus a reduction in the bases in their shares of *X* stock. For example, as of that date, *B* had a basis of $35,000 in his 30 shares of *X*'s stock (*B*'s original basis of $35,000 was increased by his $15,000 share of *X*'s Year Three net income and by his $8,000 share of *X*'s Year Four income, and was reduced by the $23,000 of the Year Four distribution to *B* that was protected by *X*'s accumulated adjustments account). So, none of the $7,000 portion of the distribution to *B* will be included in his income, and *B*'s basis in his stock will be reduced from $35,000 to $28,000. After making the distributions, *X* will have zero accumulated earnings and profits.

CHAPTER 7

TERMINATION OF ELECTION

§ 1. Revocation

A Subchapter S election can be terminated by the revocation of shareholders who hold "more than one-half of the shares of stock of the corporation on the day on which the revocation is made." If the revocation is made on or before the 15th day of the third month of a taxable year, it will be effective on the first day of that year; if the revocation is made later, it will be effective for the first day of the following taxable year. Notwithstanding the preceding rules, if the revocation specifies an effective date that is on or after the date on which the revocation is made, the effective date will be the date that is specified in the revocation. § 1362(d)(1).

§ 2. New Shareholder

A new shareholder who acquires stock after a Subchapter S election has been made does not have the unilateral power to revoke unless he owns more than one-half of the corpora-

173

tion's shares. There is no requirement that a new shareholder consent to the election. However, a shareholder (new or otherwise) can terminate the Subchapter S election by transferring one share of his stock to a person (such as a C corporation) who is not a permissible shareholder of an S corporation. As explained in section 4 below, a corporation's S status is terminated upon the date that it ceases to satisfy the requirements of Subchapter S. If such a transfer of a share of stock is bona fide, it will terminate the corporation's Subchapter S election even if that was the shareholder's purpose in making the transfer.

§ 3. Foreign Income

There is no limitation on the percentage of an S corporation's income that constitutes foreign income. That was not true prior to the adoption of the SRA. The pre-SRA rules had restricted an S corporation's foreign receipts to no more than 80 percent of its gross receipts.

§ 4. Cessation of Qualification as S Corporation

A corporation's election will terminate at any time that it ceases to qualify as an S corporation. For example, the issuing of a second class of stock or the acquisition of any of its stock by a C corporation will terminate the election.

The termination is effective on and after the date on which the corporation ceases to qualify. § 1362(d)(2). Such a termination will occur whether the terminating event is deliberate or unintentional. However, in certain circumstances, the Commissioner will exempt an S corporation from having its status terminated by an inadvertent event.

If (1) the terminating event was inadvertent, (2) within a reasonable period of time after discovery of the terminating event, steps are taken to bring the corporation into conformity with the S corporation requirements, and (3) each person who was a shareholder during the period that the corporation otherwise had lost its status as an S corporation consents to adjustments to such shareholder's income as are required by the Commissioner to provide equivalent tax consequences to that which the shareholder would have incurred if the corporation had never lost its S corporation status, then the corporation will be treated as if it had continued to qualify as an S corporation (i.e., as if a termination had not occurred). § 1362(f). Except for certain automatic relief that is afforded where the termination is attributable to the failure to file a timely election for a trust to be treated as a QSST, such relief must be obtained through a private letter ruling from the Internal Revenue Service.

§ 5. New Election After Termination

If an S corporation's status is terminated, the corporation (or a successor corporation) is barred from making a new election for S corporation treatment for a taxable year that begins prior to the fifth taxable year after the year for which the termination was first effective—i.e., the election is not available for a five-year period. The Commissioner can waive that bar and grant permission to a corporation to elect S corporation status prior to the expiration of the five-year period when the Commissioner deems it appropriate. § 1362(g). The Commissioner is not likely to consent to an early election if the termination was deliberate.

The five-year prohibition against making an election does not apply if either: (1) the termination of an election for S status is intentionally revoked by the shareholders in such manner that Subchapter S is not permitted to operate for the first day on which the election would otherwise be effective, or (2) if the corporation fails to meet the definition of a small business corporation on the first day on which the election was scheduled to be effective. Treas. Reg. § 1.1362–5(c).

§ 6. S Termination Year

A taxable year in which an election for Subchapter S treatment is terminated (other than one that terminates on the first day of the taxable year) is called an "S termination year." § 1362(e)(4). An S termination year is divided into two short years. The portion of the S termination year that ends on the day prior to the day on which the termination occurred is called an "S short year," and the remainder of the S termination year is called a "C short year." § 1362(e)(1). Subject to certain exceptions, the tax items of a corporation for the S termination year are allocated pro rata between the S short year and the C short year according to the relative lengths of those two periods. § 1362(e)(2). The division of an S termination year into two short years does not affect the taxable year of a shareholder in which the corporation's tax items are to be reported.

The tax items of the corporation are divided into two general categories. One category consists of all the tax items that are required by § 1366(a)(1)(A) to be identified and listed separately. The second category consists of the rest of the tax items, which are collectively referred to as "nonseparately computed income or loss." § 1362(e)(2).

Instead of a pro rata allocation, at the corporation's election, the allocation of tax items will be made under normal accounting rules according to the actual amounts incurred in each of those short years if consents to a normal accounting allocation are obtained from all persons who were shareholders at any time during the S short year and from all persons who were shareholders on the first day of the C short year. § 1362(e)(3). This method of allocation is sometimes referred to as the "interim closing method." A consent is not required of a person who became a shareholder after the first day of the C short year.

If, during the S termination year, there is a sale or exchange of 50 percent or more of the corporation's stock, the tax items must be allocated under normal accounting rules rather than pro rata. § 1362(e)(6)(D). If stock is sold or exchanged during the S termination year, any subsequent sale or exchange of that same stock is not taken into account for this purpose. Treas. Reg. § 1.1362–3(b)(3). In other words, there will be no double counting when the same shares are sold more than once during the same year.

If any of the stock of an S corporation target is acquired by a C corporation during a taxable year of the target, the Subchapter S election will be terminated as of the date of purchase since the electing corporation (the target) will have a C corporate shareholder as of that date; and an S corporation is not permitted to have a C corporation as a shareholder. As previously noted, the resulting S termination year will be divided into two short years.

If the number of shares purchased by the C corporation is sufficient to qualify for § 338 treatment and if the C corporation elects under § 338(g) to treat the acquisition as a purchase of assets, the target is deemed to have sold all of its assets during the S termination year. (As we have previously noted, § 338 treatment is also available when the S corporation is the acquiring corporation, but this discussion focuses only on the tax consequences when the S corporation is the target corporation.) Section 1362(e)(6)(C) provides that the pro rata allocation is not used to allocate any gain recognized by the target on the constructive sale of its assets. The House Report on the 1984 TRA states that the gain recognized by the target on a § 338 constructive sale of its assets will be allocated to the C short year. Since, under § 338(a), the deemed sale of the target's assets takes place on the close of the day on which its stock was purchased and since the target did not qualify as an S corporation on that date, all of the gain from the deemed sale is allocated to the C short year.

When the acquiring C corporation makes a unilateral election under § 338(g)—as contrasted with a joint election under § 338(h)(10)—the S corporation will actually have two C short years. The first C short year will commence and end on the acquisition date and the activities of the former S corporation on that date and all gain recognized from the

§ 338 election will be reported in that C short year. This will prevent the shareholders of the S corporation from being required to report the § 338 gain resulting from an election by the acquiring corporation in which they did not participate. The second C short year will begin on the day after the acquisition date and continue until the end of the taxable year and will reflect all activities of the corporation during that period. Treas. Reg. § 1.338–10(a)(3). On the other hand, if the election is a § 338(h)(10) election made jointly by the acquiring corporation and by all of the shareholders of the S corporation, the transaction is characterized as a sale of all the S corporation's assets occurring during the S short year, with any gain taxable to the S corporation or the S corporation's shareholders in the same manner as if the S corporation had actually sold its assets on the acquisition date. Treas. Reg. § 1.338(h)(10)–1(d)(4). For a § 338(h)(10) election to apply to a corporation's purchase of an S corporation's stock, *all* of the S corporation's shareholders, including shareholders who did not sell their stock to the acquiring corporation, must consent. Treas. Reg. § 1.338(h)(10)–1(c)(3).

If any shareholder terminates his entire interest in an S corporation during a taxable year and if the corporation's S election is not terminated thereby, the corporation and the "affected shareholders" can elect under § 1377(a)(2) to have that taxable year treated as two short taxable years, the first of which ends on the close of the day on which the shareholder's interest is terminated. This division into two short years applies only for making allocations to the "affected shareholders;" and so the determination of allocations to other shareholders of the corporation is not affected by the election. Both short years will be subject to Subchapter S. This election is sometimes referred to as a "terminating election," and the shareholder whose interest in the corporation is terminated is sometimes referred to as a "terminating shareholder."

If no shares of the shareholder whose interest was terminated were transferred to the S corporation during that year, the "affected shareholders" consist of the terminating shareholder and all persons to whom he transferred stock during the taxable year. If the terminating shareholder transferred any stock to the corporation during that year, then all persons who were shareholders during any part of the taxable year are "affected shareholders." Once made, a terminating election is irrevocable. § 1377(a)(2); Treas. Reg. § 1.1377–1(b).

If a valid terminating election is made, in making allocations to the affected shareholders for that year, the corporation must divide its tax items between the two short years according to its normal method of accounting (i.e., the allocation must be made according to the interim closing method). Treas. Reg. § 1.1377–

1(b)(3). If the same events cause both a termination of a shareholder's entire interest and also a "qualifying termination" that authorizes an election under Treas. Reg. § 1.1368–1(g)(2) to divide the corporation's taxable year into two, the § 1377(a)(2) provision has priority, and the election can be made only under that provision. Treas. Reg. §§ 1.1368–1(g)(2)(iv), 1.1377–1(b)(1). The qualifying termination provision is discussed at Section 2 of Chapter 6, supra.

(a) Tax Treatment of an S Termination Year

The normal Subchapter S provisions apply to the S short year of an S termination year. In order to maintain the progressivity built into the corporate tax structure, the taxable income of the C short year is annualized by multiplying that income by the number of days in the S termination year and then dividing the product by the number of days in the C short year. The corporation's tax liability for the C short year is equal to the income tax that would be due on the annualized income, multiplied by the ratio of the number of days in the C short year to the number of days in the S termination year. § 1362(e)(5). Also, only a percentage of the alternative minimum tax that otherwise would be payable on the annualized income for the C short year will be payable.

For purposes of determining the exhaustion of a carryover loss or credit, the two short years are treated as a single taxable year. § 1362(e)(6)(A).

Ex.   Since its incorporation, *X* Corporation has had 100 shares of common stock outstanding, 50 of which were owned by *A*, 40 of which were owned by *B*, and 10 of which were owned by *C*. *A*, *B* and *C* are unrelated individuals who report their incomes on a calendar year basis. *X* also reports its income on a calendar year basis. From its incorporation in Year One until May 26, Year Four, *X* operated as an S corporation. Year Four was not a leap year.

On May 27, Year Four, *C* sold his 10 shares of *X* stock to the *Y* Corporation, an unrelated *C* corporation. This sale terminated the Subchapter S election for *X*. Year Four is an S termination year. The period from January 1 to May 26, Year Four is an S short year, and the period from May 27 to December 31, Year Four is a C short year. In Year Four, *X* had no separately allocable items of income, deduction or credit; all of *X*'s taxable income constituted nonseparately computed income under § 1366(a)(2).

In Year Four, *X* had taxable income of $80,000, none of which was comprised of capital gains or losses. With the consent of shareholders *A*, *B*, *C*, and *Y*, *X* made a valid election to allocate the taxable income of X for the S termination year between the S short year and the C short year according to normal accounting rules (i.e., the "interim closing method") as permitted by § 1362(e)(3). Under that method, $20,000 of taxable income was allocated to the S short year, and $60,000 was allocated to the C short year.

There were 219 days in the C short year, and that constitutes 6/10 (or 60%) of the 365 days in the S termination year. The $60,000 of taxable income that is allocated to the C short year is annualized by multiplying that amount times 365 and dividing it by 219 as follows:

$$\frac{\$60,000 \times 365}{219} = \$100,000$$

The next step is to determine the corporate tax on $100,000 at current rates. At this writing the corporate tax on $100,000 of taxable income is $22,250.

Finally, since the number of days in the C short year comprises 60 percent of the number of days in the S termination year, the tax payable for the C short year is equal to 60 percent of the $22,250 tax on the annualized income for that short year. Thus, the tax payable for the C short year is $13,350 (i.e., 60% x $22,250).

The $20,000 of X's taxable income that is allocated to the corporation's S short year is allocated among X's three share-holders (A, B and C) according to normal Subchapter S allocation rules.

§ 7. Passive Investment Income Causing Termination of a Subchapter S Election

Unless an S corporation has accumulated e *and* p, there is no penalty for having passive investment income—i.e., such income does not cause the termination of the election nor does it cause the imposition of any federal income taxes on the S corporation. You will recall that there are only two circumstances in which an S corporation can have accumulated e *and* p: (1) it accumulated e *and* p during a time when it was a C corporation, or (2) it acquired the e *and* p of another corporation as a consequence of an acquisitive reorganization or a liquidation of that corporation.

A Subchapter S election will be terminated if:

(1) the corporation had accumulated earnings and profits at the close of each of three consecutive taxable years in each of which it was an S corporation; and

(2) in each of such taxable years, more than 25 percent of the corporation's gross receipts was passive investment income (as defined in § 1362(d)(3)(C)).

A taxable year that began prior to 1982 is not taken into account. A termination that is caused by the corporation's having passive investment income takes place on the first day of the taxable year following the close of the third consecutive year referred to above. § 1362(d)(3).

"Passive investment income" is defined in § 1362(d)(3)(C). See also Treas. Reg. § 1.1362–2(c)(5). In general, subject to exceptions described in § 1362(d)(3)(C)(ii), (iii), and (iv), passive investment income means gross receipts from royalties, rents, dividends, interest, annuities, and gains from the sales or exchanges of stocks or securities. The gross receipts from tax-exempt interest is included in the corporation's passive investment income. Treas. Reg. § 1.1362–2(c)(5)(ii).

Rents derived from the active conduct of the trade or business of renting property are not treated as passive investment income. Consequently, for the purpose of determining "passive investment income," the term "rent" does *not* include rents received from the rental of property where the corporation either provides significant services or incurs substantial costs in conducting a rental business. Id. In most cases, rent received under a net lease will constitute passive investment income. Id. The supply of maid service, for example, constitutes a significant service; whereas the furnishing of heat and light and the cleaning of public entrances does not. Receipts for the letting of rooms in a hotel, motel or boarding house typically will not constitute rent since significant services usually are provided.

§ 8. Inadvertent Termination or Failure to Qualify

If an election for Subchapter S status is invalid because the corporation failed to qualify for that status or because timely consents were not filed, or if a Subchapter S election was terminated, and if the Service determines that the circumstances resulting in that invalidity or termination were inadvertent, and if, within a reasonable time after those circumstances were discovered, steps were taken to comply with the requirements for S corporation classification or to obtain the consents of the shareholders, the corporation will be treated as an S corporation during the period specified by the Service, provided that the corporation and all persons who were shareholders during that period consent to such adjustments as are required by the Service to conform tax consequences with the S corporation status. § 1362(f).

CHAPTER 8

TAXATION OF PASSIVE INVESTMENT INCOME

As noted in Section 7 of Chapter 7, an S corporation that has accumulated earnings and profits and has a substantial portion of its gross receipts from passive investment income is given three consecutive years to get its house in order before the election will be terminated. But, in addition to the termination provision, a corporation is subject to tax consequences in any taxable year in which a significant percentage of its gross receipts is passive investment income if it also has accumulated *e and p* at the end of that taxable year. Section 1375 imposes a tax on an S corporation for any taxable year in which it has both:

(1) accumulated earnings and profits at the close of that taxable year; and

(2) gross receipts more than 25 percent of which are passive investment income.

The § 1375 tax is computed by multiplying the "excess net passive income" by the highest ordinary income tax rate that is applicable to corporations (currently, that rate is 35 percent). By "ordinary" rate, we refer to the corporate income tax rates exclusive of surtaxes. The "net passive income" of a corporation is the difference between its passive investment income (as defined in § 1362(d)(3)(C)), and the corporation's deductions that are directly connected with the production of such income (other than net operating loss deductions and certain special deductions allowable only to corporations such as the dividend-received deduction). § 1375(b)(2). The "excess net passive income" is an amount that has the same ratio to net passive income as the excess of passive investment income over 25 percent of gross receipts has to the corporation's passive investment income.

The amount of excess net passive income for a taxable year cannot exceed a modified version of the corporation's taxable income for that year. For this purpose, the corporation's taxable income is computed by excluding all net operating loss carryovers and carrybacks and by excluding the deductions allowed by §§ 243–247, and 249. § 1375(b)(1)(B). Note that the special calculation of taxable income of an S corporation that ordinarily is required by § 1363(b) does not apply to the taxable income limitation of this section, which instead provides its own special definition.

It may be helpful to express the manner in which "excess net passive income" (ENPI) is determined as a formula. In the following formula:

ENPI = excess net passive income

PII = passive investment income

NPI = net passive income

GR = gross receipts

$$\text{ENPI} = \frac{\text{PII—25\% of GR}}{\text{PII}} \times \text{NPI}$$

Ex. (1)   *X* Corporation conducted a personal service business as a C corporation in Year One, but it became an S corporation beginning January 1, Year Two. *X* reports its income on a calendar year basis. In Year Two, *X* had gross receipts of $100,000 of which $37,500 constitute interest from bonds of publicly held corporations and $62,500 constitute receipts from the conduct of a personal service business. Individual *A* is the sole shareholder of *X*. *X* made no distributions to its shareholder in Year Two. *X* had deductible expenses in Year Two of $25,000 of which $7,500 is attributable to the interest it earned. The remaining $17,500 of deductible expenses are attributable to the receipts from the personal service business. At the beginning of Year Two, *X* had accumulated *e and p* of $18,000.

Of *X*'s gross receipts, only the interest it received constitutes passive investment income. *X*'s net passive income for Year

Two is $30,000 (i.e., $37,500 interest minus the $7,500 of deductible expenses that are directly attributable thereto). X's passive investment income ($37,500) exceeds 25 percent of its gross receipts for that year (25% x $100,000 = $25,000) by $12,500. X's excess net passive income is determined by multiplying the net passive income ($30,000) by a fraction the numerator of which is the passive investment income in excess of 25 percent of X's gross receipts ($12,500) and the denominator of which is X's passive investment income ($37,500). So, in tabular form,

$$\frac{12,500}{37,500} \times \$30,000 = \$10,000$$

(*excess net passive income*)

Since the amount of X's taxable income for Year Two ($75,000) is greater than its excess net passive income, the tax is determined by applying the tax rate to the ENPI. The $10,000 of excess net passive income is taxed to X at a 35 percent rate. This provides a tax of $3,500.

The $37,500 of interest income of X that is passed through to A is reduced by the $3,500 tax that X incurred under § 1375(a), and so A will report $34,000 of interest income from the S corporation. Note that if X's $37,500 of passive investment income had consisted of several items (such as interest and royalty income) instead of being a single item, each such item that passed through to a shareholder would be reduced by its pro rata share of the $3,500 tax that was imposed on *X* by § 1375. *X*'s deductions also pass through to *A*.

Ex. (2)   The same facts as those stated in **Ex. (1)** except that on December 30, Year Two, *X* distributed $18,000 to *A*. *X* elected under § 1368(e)(3) to preclude the application of the accumulated adjustments account rules to distributions made by *X* in Year Two, and *A* consented to that election. Accordingly, the $18,000 that *X* distributed to *A* on December, 30, Year Two, constitutes dividend income to *A*; and by the end of that year, *X* had no accumulated earnings and profits. Since *X* had no accumulated earnings and profits at the end of its taxable year, no tax is imposed on *X*'s excess net passive income.

It is possible that gain recognized by an S corporation from the disposition of an asset could constitute both passive investment income and a "recognized built-in gain" as defined in § 1374(d)(3). To prevent a double tax, the amount of an S corporation's passive investment income is determined by excluding any of the corporation's recognized built-in gains and losses that are recognized during the "recognition period." § 1375(b)(4). The meaning of the terms "recognized built-in gains," "recognized built-in loss," and "recognition period'' are explained in Chapter 9, infra in the discussion of § 1374.

The Commissioner (by delegation from the Secretary) is authorized by § 1375(d) to excuse an S corporation from a tax on its passive investment income if it is established to the satisfaction of the Commissioner that:

(1) the corporation had determined in good faith that it had no accumulated earnings and profits at the close of the taxable year in question; and

(2) the corporation distributed its accumulated earnings and profits within a reasonable period of time after it was determined that the corporation had them.

CHAPTER 9

TAXATION OF BUILT–IN GAINS

§ 1. In General

While an S corporation generally does not incur federal income tax liability, there are several exceptions to that general rule. One exception, discussed in Chapter 8, supra, is the tax imposed by § 1375 on an S corporation's "excess net passive income." Another major exception is that § 1374 taxes an S corporation on its "net recognized built-in gain." The tax rate imposed by both provisions is the maximum ordinary rate on corporate income, which currently is a 35 percent rate. By "ordinary" rate, we refer to the corporate income tax rates exclusive of surtaxes. We will explain in this Chapter the meaning of the term, net recognized built-in gain, the limitations on its amount, and how the tax operates. First, let us consider the tax consequences of an S corporation's distributing appreciated property to a shareholder.

In the 1986 TRA, when Congress repudiated the *General Utilities* doctrine, Congress sought to ensure that a corporate level tax will be imposed on the appreciation of corporate assets. Thus, if a C corporation distributes an appreciated asset as a § 301 distribution or as a liquidating distribution, the corporation will recognize gain under § 311(b) or § 336(a). The same recognition provisions apply to distributions made by an S corporation. § 1371(a).

The S corporation may or may not be taxed on such recognized gain; in either event, the gain will pass through to the S corporation's shareholders. If the gain constitutes a built-in gain that is recognized during a recognition period, it may be taxed to the S corporation under § 1374. Ordinarily, the "recognition period" is the 10–year period that begins on the first day of the first year that the corporation became an S corporation. § 1374(d)(7). As discussed in Chapter 8, supra, even if the gain does not constitute a recognized built-in gain or if it was not recognized during the recognition period, it nevertheless may be taxed to the S corporation if it constitutes passive investment income and if the requirements of § 1375 are satisfied.

If the S corporation is taxed on such gain, then, depending upon whether the gain is taxed under § 1374 or § 1375, the tax either will pass through to the shareholders as a loss or will reduce the amount of the gain that passes through to the shareholders. § 1366(f)(2), (3). If both § 1374 and § 1375 would otherwise apply to the same gain or loss recognized by the S corporation, the built-in gain tax of § 1374 has priority. § 1375(b)(4).

§ 2. Purpose and Operation of § 1374 Tax

In the absence of a remedial provision, a C corporation that has appreciated assets could avoid the imposition of a corporate tax on that appreciation by making an election to become an S corporation. Once the election became effective, the corporation's recognition of gain would be passed through to its shareholders and therefore would be taxed only once, at individual rates. Without the S election, the gain would have been taxed twice—once at the corporate level and again at the individual shareholder's level when the proceeds are distributed to the shareholders. To discourage the use of the Subchapter S election as a device for escaping corporate taxation of appreciation that arose prior to the effective date of the election, Congress imposed a corporate tax on the "net recognized built-in gain" of an S corporation when it is recognized within a specified period. This tax is set forth in § 1374.

If left unchecked, an S corporation could be used in another manner to permit a C corporation to escape double taxation on the appreciation of its assets. An S corporation could acquire appreciated assets of a C corporation in a nonrecognition, carryover basis transaction so that any gain on the subsequent disposition of those assets would be recognized by the S corporation and passed through to its share-holders—thereby escaping double taxation. To prevent that abuse, such assets are subject to the § 1374 tax on built-in gains. § 1374(d)(8). In this book, assets that were acquired by an S corporation from a C corporation in a carryover basis transaction are sometimes referred to as "C assets."

In this light, the § 1374 tax represents an effort to discourage corporations eligible to make a Subchapter S election from using the S corporation rules to circumvent the 1986 re-peal of the *General Utilities* doctrine. Other-wise, such corporations could readily escape the double-tax regime of corporate taxation by simply electing S status just prior to the sale of their assets. As it is, of course, the double tax regime for C corporations can still be avoided by electing S corporation status if the parties have the patience to wait 10 years before dis-posing of assets that appreciated while held by the C corporation. Thus, the § 1374 tax will not always prevent taxpayers from using the S corporation regime to avoid *General Utilities* repeal. In most cases, however, the ten-year waiting period will at least provide a substan-tial impediment to using the Subchapter S election for this purpose.

To some degree, the § 1375 tax on excessive passive investment income serves a complementary purpose to that of § 1374. Without that tax, it would be easier for a C corporation to avoid the shareholder-level tax on its undistributed C corporation *e and p* by electing S status and investing its *e and p* indefinitely, or at least until its principal shareholder(s) died. In the meantime, the shareholders could enjoy the fruits of investing the C corporation *e and p* without incurring a shareholder-level tax on them. The corporation could then distribute the pro rata share of those earnings to the shareholder's estate without tax as a result of the stepped up basis in the shareholder's stock that occurs at death.

Of course, such use of an S corporation is still tolerated to some extent even under § 1375, but only to the degree that the investment earnings of the S corporation with accumulated *e and p* do not exceed 25 percent of gross receipts. Thus, as with § 1374, § 1375 discourages but does not prevent the use of an S corporation to circumvent the double tax regime that otherwise applies to C corporations. In this respect, the § 1375 tax, as well as the required termination of S corporation status following three consecutive years of excessive passive income by an S corporation with accumulated *e and p*, can be viewed as a way to discourage the use of an S corporation to circumvent the accumulated earnings tax and the personal holding company tax, neither of which applies to S corporations. § 1363(a).

Consistent with its purpose to discourage circumvention of *General Utilities* repeal, the § 1374 tax generally applies to gain on corporate assets that accrued during the time the corporation was a C corporation or during the time the assets were held by a C corporation. Thus, any gain that can be shown to have accrued to the corporation after the S election was effective ordinarily will not be subject to the tax. As discussed below, however, the S corporation will bear the burden of proof to show how much, if any, of the gain from the disposition of corporate assets during the ten-year "recognition period" accrued during the time the corporation was a C corporation in order to exclude the remainder of the gain. For that reason, it is common for tax advisers to recommend that, upon the making of an S election, a former C corporation obtain a professional and contemporaneous appraisal of its major tangible and intangible assets. Although such an appraisal will not necessarily prevent the Internal Revenue Service from disputing the results of that appraisal for purposes of determining the "built-in gain" calculation, it will place the Service at a substantial evidentiary disadvantage in any such controversy because the taxpayer will have an invaluable item of proof that the Service will not be able to replicate—a contemporaneous appraisal.

In examining the built-in gains tax, it is best to begin with an analysis of the definitions of the key terminology used to determine the tax. We will describe each of those terms below and discuss the role that each plays, both separately and in conjunction with each other, in the application of the built-in gain tax. We will then conclude with a brief summary of how those terms work in tandem to determine the § 1374 tax.

(a) Recognition Period

The "recognition period" of an S corporation is ordinarily the ten-year period beginning with the date on which the Subchapter S election of the corporation first became effective. § 1374(d)(7). However, in the case of any assets that the S corporation acquired from a C corporation in a transaction in which the basis of the asset to the S corporation is determined in whole or in part by reference to the basis the asset had in the hands of the C corporation, the recognition period for that asset is the ten-year period beginning on the date on which the S corporation acquired it. § 1374(d)(8)(B). Thus, it is possible for there to be one recognition period that applies with respect to certain assets of an S corporation and other recognition periods that apply with respect to other assets of the S corporation. For convenience, we sometimes refer to an asset that was acquired from a C corporation in a carryover basis transaction as a "C asset."

(b) Built-in Gain and Loss

For convenience, we refer herein to the excess of the fair market value of an asset of an S corporation on the day on which the Subchapter S election first became effective, or on the date the S corporation acquired the asset from a C corporation in a carryover basis transaction (a C asset), over the adjusted basis that the S corporation had in the asset at that date as the "built-in gain" of that asset. The excess of adjusted basis over fair market value of an asset on the dates referenced above is referred to herein as the "built-in loss" of that asset. Although "built-in gain" and "built-in loss" are not defined terms for purposes of the statute, we find it convenient to use these terms as short-cuts for the purpose of describing the terms that are defined in the statute and are used for purposes of determining the § 1374 tax.

(c) Net Unrealized Built-in Gain

The "net unrealized built-in gain" of an S corporation is the excess of the aggregate fair market values of the corporation's assets at the date that the corporation's Subchapter S election first became effective over the aggregate adjusted bases that the S corporation had in those assets at that date. § 1374(d)(1) and

(8)(B). In addition, if the S corporation acquires any C assets in a nonrecognition transaction, there will be a separate net unrealized built-in gain determined for each transaction in which such C assets are acquired. For this purpose, both the aggregate adjusted bases of the acquired assets and their aggregate fair market value will be determined as of the acquisition date. See § 1374(d)(8) and Treas. Reg. § 1.1374–8(e) Exs. 1 and 2.

Treasury Regulation § 1.1374–3(a) states that an S corporation's net unrealized built-in gain is equal to the amount that would have been realized on the first day of the recognition period if the corporation had sold all of its assets at fair market value to an unrelated person who assumed all of its liabilities, decreased by the sum of: (i) any liability that would be included in the determination above of the amount realized, but only to the extent that the liability would entitle the corporation to a deduction when paid, and (ii) the aggregate adjusted bases of the corporation's assets on the first day of the recognition period. The regulation provides two adjustments in determining net unrealized built-in gain. If on the first day of the recognition period, the corporation was subject to unrecognized § 481 adjustments, those § 481 adjustments will be added (if they represent income adjustments) or deducted (if they represent deductible adjustments). Any recognized built-in loss that would not be allowed as a deduction on a sale because of §§ 382, 383 or 384 (those are limitations on the availability of favorable tax items acquired by a corporation in a reorganization or certain other nonrecognition transactions) will be added.

As previously noted, the built-in gain tax of § 1374 applies to the recognition of gain or loss of C assets during the recognition period for those assets; and each pool of C assets that were acquired in the same nonrecognition transaction has its own recognition period and net unrealized built-in gain. Similarly, the net recognized built-in gain is determined separately for each pool. The § 1374 tax is applied separately to the separate net recognized built-in gain for each pool of C assets that were acquired in the same nonrecognition transaction and applied separately to the net recognized gain of the pool of assets that the corporation held at the time that its S corporation election became effective. Treas. Reg. § 1.1374–8(c). The recognized built-in gain or loss of one pool of assets does not affect the net recognized built-in gain of other pools of assets.

As described in section 2(f) below, there are two limitations on a corporation's net recognized built-in gain—the taxable income limitation and the net unrealized built-in gain limitation. The regulations require that the taxable income limitation be apportioned among the separate pools of net recognized built-in gains for that year according to the ratio of those recognized built-in gains. Treas. Reg. § 1.1374–8(d). The regulations make no provision for an allocation of the corporation's net unrealized built in gain limitation. That seems appropriate in light of the fact, noted above, that the statute and regulations contemplate that each separate pool of assets will have its own separate net unrealized built-in gain limitation. See Treas. Reg. §§ 1.1374–3(b) and 1.1374–8(e) Exs. 1 and 2.

If a corporation has an item that would be a recognized built-in gain or loss if properly recognized during the recognition period, the corporation's net unrealized built in gain is adjusted for those amounts at the time that the corporation's S election became effective or at the time that the corporation acquired the asset in a nonrecognition transaction. § 1374(d)(5).

(d) Recognized Built-in Gain

The "recognized built-in gain" of an S corporation is the amount of built-in gain recognized on the disposition of an asset by the S corporation in a taxable year that is within the "recognition period." The presumption is that any gain recognized by an S corporation on the disposition of an asset during the recognition period is a recognized built-in gain unless the S corporation establishes either that that asset was not held by the corporation at the date that the Subchapter S election became effective and was not a C asset or that the built-in gain for that asset is less than the gain recognized on its disposition. § 1374(d)(3), (8). In other words, any gain recognized by an S corporation during a recognition period will be treated as a recognized built-in gain except to the extent that the corporation can prove that all or part of the gain is not. A corporation's recognized built-in gains for a taxable year within the recognition period also include any item of income that is properly taken into account for that taxable year and that is attributable to periods prior to the first taxable year in which the Subchapter S election became effective (i.e., prior to the beginning of the recognition period). Similarly, as noted below, a corporation's recognized built-in loss for a taxable year will include any deduction for that year that is attributable to periods prior to the recognition period. § 1374(d)(5). This provision for such income or deductions is sometimes referred to as the "accrual method provision."

The regulations elaborate on the meaning of the accrual method provision. Treas. Reg. § 1.1374–4(b) states that, as to income, this provision applies only to an item of income that is taken into account during the recognition period and that would have been included in gross income before the recognition period if the taxpayer had been using the accrual method of accounting. As to an item of deduction that is attributable to a pre-recognition period year, that same regulation states that such items are included as a recognized built-in loss only if the item is properly deductible during the recognition period and would have been properly allowed against gross income before the recognition period by a taxpayer using the accrual method. Obviously then, the accrual method provision does not apply if the corporation was using the accrual method of accounting when the item of income or deduction was incurred.

If an accrual method item would produce a gain if recognized during a recognition period, it will increase the corporation's net unrealized built-in gain. § 1374(d)(5)(C).

If a transaction of the S corporation is covered both by the accrual method provision and by another provision dealing with recognized built-in gain, the other provision takes priority and is the one that is applied. See Treas. Reg. § 1.1374–4(b)(3), Ex. (1).

The following examples, which are drawn from the regulations, illustrate how the accrual method provision operates.

Ex. (1)   X was a calendar year C corporation using the cash method of accounting. X elected to become an S corporation on January 1, Year Three. At that time, X had accounts receivable of $50,000 in which it had a basis of zero. The fair market value of the accounts receivable at that time was $40,000. While the regulatory examples do not address the question of how the accounts receivable will affect the corporation's net unrealized built-in gain, the authors believe that the amount of the receivables that is added to the corporation's net unrealized built-in gain is $50,000—the amount of recognized built-in gain that X would have if the receivable were properly recognized during the recognition period. § 1374(d)(5)(C).

In Year Four, *X* collects the entire $50,000 of the receivables. The entire $50,000 is a recognized built-in gain because that amount would have been included in *X*'s gross income prior to the recognition period if X had been on the accrual method of accounting.

If instead of collecting the receivables, *X* had sold them to an unrelated person for $50,000 in Year Four, it would have recognized a gain of $50,000, but only $40,000 of that gain would have constituted recognized built-in gain. Under § 1374(d)(3), the amount of recognized built-in gain from the sale of an asset is limited to the amount of the asset's appreciation (i.e., the difference between the asset's value and its basis) as of the beginning of the first taxable year in which the corporation was an S corporation. The gain recognized on the sale of the receivables is dealt with in Treas. Reg. § 1.1374–4(a) (which relates to

§ 1374(d)(3) and (4)), and that provision takes priority. Treas. Reg. § 1.1374–4(b)(3), Ex. (1). Since the accrual method provision concerning the recognition of previously accruable items does not apply, then the normal restriction is applicable—i.e., that a recognized built-in gain on an item cannot exceed the difference between the fair market value of that item at the beginning of the recognition period and the basis of the item at that time. Treas. Reg. § 1.1374–4(b)(3), Ex. (1).

Ex. (2)   *Y* corporation was a C corporation, using the accrual method, that elected to become an S corporation as of January 1, Year Three. In Year Two, *Y* had received $3,000 for services to be rendered in the following year. *Y* elected under Rev. Proc. 2004–34 to defer the recognition of the $3,000 income until Year Three. In Year Three, *Y* will recognize $3,000 of income; but none of it will constitute recognized built-in gain since it was not income that would have been recognized in a pre-recognition period by an accrual method taxpayer. Treas. Reg. § 1.1374–4(b)(3), Ex. (4).

When an asset is sold prior to or during the recognition period, and when gain from that sale is reported under the installment method, the installment gain from that sale that is reported during or after the recognition period can be subject to tax as built-in gain under § 1374. Treas. Reg. § 1.1374–4(h). If the asset was sold during the recognition period, the gain that is recognized should be limited to the built-in gain of that asset at the beginning of the recognition period or when it was acquired in a nonrecognition transaction from a C corporation.

The recognized built-in gain for a corporation can be increased by a carryover from a prior year of the amount of the corporation's net recognized built-in gain that escaped taxation because of the taxable income limitation, which is discussed below. § 1374(d)(2)(B). This carryover provision is discussed below in connection with the explanation of the meaning of the term "net recognized built-in gain."

(e) Recognized Built-in Loss

Part of the determination of a "net recognized built-in gain" is a netting of recognized built-in gains and losses for a taxable year that began within the recognition period applicable to the assets in question. The manner in which a recognized built-in gain for a taxable year is determined is described above. A "recognized built-in loss" is any loss recognized by an S corporation during the applicable recognition period on the disposition of an asset that was held by the S corporation at the date on which the applicable recognition period began, but only to the extent of the excess of the adjusted basis that the corporation had in such asset at the date on which the recognition period began over the fair market value of the asset at that date (i.e., only to the extent of the built-in loss of that asset). The S corporation has the burden of establishing that it held the asset at the operative date and the burden of establishing the spread between basis and value at that date. § 1374(d)(4). Note that, when gain is recognized during the recognition period, the burden is on the taxpayer to show that the gain was not part of a built-in gain; but, if a loss is recognized during the recognition period, the burden is on the taxpayer to show that the loss was part of a built-in loss.

A recognized loss on the disposition of a C asset also will be a recognized built-in loss to the extent that the corporation can prove that the loss was built-in at the time that the corporation acquired the C asset. You will recall that each pool of C assets that were acquired in the same transaction is treated as a separate pool of assets to which § 1374 can apply.

A corporation's recognized built-in loss for a taxable year within the recognition period also includes any amount that is allowable as a deduction for such year (determined without regard to any carryover) and that is attributable to periods prior to the recognition period. § 1374(d)(5)(B). This is another aspect of the rule referred to as the "accrual method provision." The regulations elaborate on the meaning of this accrual method provision.

The corporation's net unrealized built-in gain will be adjusted for deductions that would be added to the corporation's recognized built-in loss if properly taken into account during the recognition period. § 1374(d)(5)(C).

As to an item of deduction that is attributable to a pre-recognition period year, the regulations state that such items are included as a recognized built-in loss only if the item is properly deductible during the recognition period and would have been properly allowed against gross income before the recognition period by a taxpayer using the accrual method. Treas. Reg. § 1.1374–4(b)(2). As noted above, this provision is part of the so-called "accrual method provision." Obviously, the accrual method provision does not apply when the C corporation reported its income on the accrual method. Also, the accrual method provision does not apply if any other provision of the regulation is applicable (in other words, in the event of an overlap of regulatory provisions, the other provision takes priority). Id. For example, the accrual method provision does not apply to a loss recognized on the sale or exchange of an item since such a loss is dealt with in another paragraph of the regulations. The following example, drawn from Treas. Reg. § 1.1374–4(b)(3), Exs. (2) and (3), illustrates the meaning and operation of this regulatory provision.

Ex.   *X* was a calendar year C corporation using the cash method of accounting. In

Year One, a lawsuit was filed against X claiming $1,000,000 in damages for a tort. X became an S corporation on January 1, Year Six. In Year Six, X lost the lawsuit, paid a $500,000 judgment, and properly claimed a deduction for that amount. If, as seems likely, X would not have been allowed to accrue a deduction for its contingent liability before the beginning of the recognition period even if X had reported its income on the accrual method, the $500,000 deduction does not constitute a recognized built-in loss.

(f) Net Recognized Built-in Gain

An S corporation's "net recognized built-in gain" with respect to a taxable year in the recognition period is the amount of difference between the corporation's recognized built-in gain for such taxable year and the corporation's recognized built-in loss for such taxable year (§ 1374(d)(2)), except that such excess is reduced by any carryovers of net operating losses and capital losses that can be deducted from net recognized built-in gain in that year pursuant to § 1374(b)(2). That provision refers to carryovers from a year in which the corporation was a C corporation. In addition, certain carryover credits can reduce the § 1374 tax. § 1374(b)(3).

A corporation's net recognized built-in gain is subject to two limitations: (1) the taxable income limitation, and (2) the net unrealized built-in gain limitation.

Under the second limitation, a corporation's net recognized built-in gain for a year cannot exceed the difference between the corporation's net unrealized built-in gain and the aggregate net recognized built-in gain for all prior taxable years that began in the recognition period. The term "net unrealized built-in gain" was defined earlier in this section. This limitation is referred to as the "net unrealized built-in gain limitation."

Under the first limitation, if an S corporation's modified taxable income for a taxable year is less than the amount of difference between its recognized built-in gains and losses for such year, then the net recognized built-in gain for that year is equal to the corporation's modified taxable income. § 1374(d)(2)(A)(ii). This is referred to as "the taxable income limitation." For this purpose, an S corporation's taxable income is determined in the normal manner that applies to C corporations except that no deduction can be taken under § 172 for a carryover or carryback of a net operating loss and no deduction can be taken under §§ 243 through 247 and 249. Note that the special computation of taxable income of an S corporation that ordinarily is required by § 1363(b) does not apply for the purpose of determining the taxable income limitation.

You will recall that if an S corporation has C assets, its assets are divided into separate pools, and the recognition period, net unrealized built-in gain, and net recognized built-in gain of each pool are determined separately. The corporation's taxable income limitation is allocated among the pools according to the amount of net recognized built-in gain in each pool for that year. Treas. Reg. § 1.1374–8(d).

If the net recognized built-in gain for a taxable year is equal to the S corporation's taxable income for that year because the taxable income limitation applies, the additional amount that would have been taxed under § 1374 if taxable income had not been the smaller figure will be carried forward and added to the corporation's recognized built-in gains for the next taxable year. § 1374(d)(2)(B). Thus, a corporation's recognized built-in gains for a taxable year include the amounts from prior years that escaped taxation because of the taxable income limitation.

This carryover is referred to as the "recognized built-in gain carryover." A recognized built-in gain carryover that is unused in one year will carryover to the next year for so long as the recognition period has not expired. There is no carryover to years that begin after the expiration of the recognition period.

Note that while the tax imposed by § 1375 on excess net passive income also contains a taxable income limitation, there is no carryover of the amount of excess net passive income that is not taxed because of that limitation. § 1375(b)(1)(B).

If left unchecked, shareholders of a C corporation could transfer depreciated assets to it shortly prior to the corporation's making a Subchapter S election in order to reduce the size of the corporation's net unrealized built-in gain. To counter this, the regulations have adopted an "anti-stuffing" rule. This rule provides that if an asset is acquired by a corporation prior to or during the recognition period for the principal purpose of avoiding the built-in gain tax, the asset and its tax attributes are ignored for most purposes concerning § 1374. Treas. Reg. § 1.1374–9.

Treas, Reg. § 1.1374–2 provides a summary of the method for determining an S corporation's net recognized built-in gain. The following summary is drawn from that regulation. A corporation's net recognized built-in gain for a taxable year is the least of:

(1) its taxable income as determined by using the rules applying to C corporations and by considering only its recognized built-in gains, its recognized built-in losses, and its recognized built-in gain carryover (this provision is referred to as "the pre-limitation amount");

(2) the taxable income limitation; or

(3) the amount by which its net unrealized built-in gain exceeds its net recognized built-in gains for all prior years ("the net unrealized built-in gain limitation").

When the taxable income limitation applies to a taxable year (so that the net recognized built-in gain for that year will be less than the pre-limitation amount), it will be necessary to determine which of the corporation's income items are included in the corporation's net recognized built-in gain and which are carried over to the next year as a recognized built-in gain carryover. The regulations state that the corporation's net recognized built-in gain consists of a ratable portion of each item of income, gain, loss, and deduction that is included in the pre-limitation amount.

(g) Asset Held by S Corporation at First Day on Which Election Became Effective

If the adjusted basis of any asset is determined in whole or in part by reference to the adjusted basis of an asset that was held by the S corporation on the first day on which its S election became effective, then such later acquired asset will be treated as having been held by the S corporation at the time that its S election first became effective. § 1374(d)(6). Similarly, if the adjusted basis of an asset is determined in whole or in part by reference to the corporation's adjusted basis in a C asset, the asset will be treated as a C asset. § 1374(d)(8).

When an S corporation sells inventory during the recognition period, it becomes necessary to determine whether the inventory that was sold was an asset that was held by the corporation on the first day of the recognition period; and, if so, the amount of built-in gain or loss that the asset had at that time. If the inventory item that was sold is deemed to have been acquired after the first day of the recognition period, the gain or loss from that sale does not constitute a recognized built-in gain or loss.

Treas. Reg. § 1.1374–7(b) states that the inventory method that an S corporation employs for tax purposes will be used to identify the items of inventory that are sold during a taxable year. Thus, if an S corporation uses the FIFO (first-in, first-out) inventory method, the oldest inventory in its stock will be deemed to be sold first, and that will cause the earliest recognition of built-in gains from the inventory held at the beginning of the recognition period. On the other hand, if the corporation uses the LIFO (last-in, first-out) method, the later acquired inventory will be deemed to have been sold first, and that will delay the recognition of built-in gains on inventory. Indeed, the LIFO method could delay the recognition of such gain to years beyond the recognition period so that they will never be subjected to the built-in gains tax.

If a C corporation was using the LIFO method prior to electing S status, that could be advantageous for built-in gains tax purposes; but the tax benefit obtained thereby is offset by the requirement that the C corporation recognize the so-called LIFO recapture amount as income in its return for its last taxable year as a C corporation. The tax on that income is payable in four equal annual installments beginning with the return for the last year in which the corporation was a C corporation. The corporation's basis in the inventory will be increased by the LIFO recapture amount. § 1363(d).

The "LIFO recapture amount" is defined in § 1363(d)(3) as the excess of the inventory amount that the corporation would have had at the close of its last taxable year as a C corporation if it had reported its inventory on the first-in, first-out (FIFO) method over the inventory amount that the corporation actually had at that date as a consequence of using the LIFO method.

If a C corporation had been using the FIFO method, despite incurring a tax on the LIFO recapture amount, it still might be advantageous for the corporation to change to the LIFO method just prior to or shortly after the effective date of an S election. In some cases, it might be advantageous for a corporation to change from the LIFO method to the FIFO method. The regulations provide that, if a corporation changes its inventory method for the principal purpose of avoiding the built-in gains tax, it must use its prior method to identify its dispositions of inventory. Treas. Reg. § 1.1374–7(b). If the corporation can provide a good business reason for changing to a different method of accounting for its inventory, it may be able to utilize that method for built-in gain purposes as well.

The regulations contain a number of provisions dealing with the circumstance where an S corporation owned a partnership interest on the first day of the recognition period and with the circumstance where an S corporation transferred property to a partnership during the recognition period as part of a nonrecognition exchange. The concern is to prevent the use of the partnership entity as a device to avoid built-in gains tax on appreciated assets. In general, the regulations accomplish this by looking through the partnership entity and treating the corporation as the owner of its share of partnership assets in certain circumstances. The manner in which this is accomplished is complex and may cause difficult administrative problems. In recognition of that difficulty, the regulations contain a *de minimis* exception that excludes from this treatment any taxable year in the recognition period in which: (1) for the entire period of that year and prior taxable years of the recognition period, the S corporation's partnership interest had a value that is less than ten percent of the partnership's capital and profits, and (2) the fair market value of the partnership interest at the beginning of the recognition period was less than $100,000. This *de minimis* exception does not apply if the S corporation formed or availed of the partnership with the principal purpose of avoiding the built-in gains tax.

Note that the regulations' treatment of an S corporation's holding of partnership interests allows for an S corporation to incur recognized built-in losses as well as gains.

For the details of the tax consequences of an S corporation's holding of a partnership interest, the reader is advised to study Treas. Reg. § 1.1374–4(i).

(h) Summary

If an S corporation has a "net recognized built-in gain" for a taxable year that began within the applicable "recognition period," § 1374 imposes a tax on such gain. The "net recognized built-in gain" in any year is the excess of the "recognized built-in gain" over the "recognized built-in loss" in that year subject to the taxable income and net unrealized built-in gain limitations. The rate of tax to be applied under this provision is the maximum ordinary income tax rate that is applicable to corporate income; currently, this rate is 35 percent. The S corporation is allowed to offset against such net recognized built-in gain net operating loss and capital loss carryovers and to offset against the § 1374 tax imposed thereon certain credits that are carried forward from years in which the corporation was a C corporation. The corporation is also allowed to reduce its § 1374 tax by the fuel credit provided by § 34. § 1374(b)(2) and (3).

With one exception, if a corporation and its predecessor corporations, if any, have been S corporations since their inception, the § 1374 tax does not apply. § 1374(c)(1). Thus, the tax applies only if the S corporation or a predecessor corporation had once been a C corporation. An exception to that exclusion is that the tax can be imposed if an S corporation acquired an appreciated asset in a tax-free exchange and if the S corporation's basis in the acquired asset is determined in whole or in part by reference to the basis of that asset (or other property) in the hands of a C corporation. In this book, we refer to such assets as "C assets." If gain from a C asset is recognized in a year that began within a recognition period (which for this purpose is the ten-year period beginning with the acquisition of the C asset from the C corporation), it can be taxed, and it will not matter whether the S corporation that recognized the gain had been an S corporation since its inception. § 1374(d)(8).

An S corporation's net recognized built-in gain for a taxable year cannot exceed the difference between the corporation's net unrealized built-in gain and the aggregate amount of net built-in gains that the corporation had recognized in prior years of its recognition period. § 1374(c)(2). That provision, which is referred to as the "net unrealized built-in gain limitation," prevents the S corporation from being taxed more than once on its built-in gains. This provision is applied separately to each pool of C assets that the S corporation acquired, using the separate recognition period and net unrealized built-in gain that apply to that pool of C assets. It might appear that this limitation means that the aggregate amount of built-in gain that can be recognized cannot exceed the amount that was built-in at the time that the corporation first obtained its S corporation status or at the time the S corporation acquired C assets. However, that limitation may not be useful if the S corporation cannot carry its burden of proving the amount of net unrecognized built-in gain that existed at the time that the Subchapter S election first became effective or the relevant pool of C assets was acquired.

An S corporation's net recognized built-in gain for a taxable year also cannot exceed a modified version of the corporation's taxable income for that year. § 1374(d)(2)(A)(ii). This is referred to as "the taxable income limitation." For this purpose, the S corporation's taxable income is modified in the same manner as is employed in determining the taxable income limitation on the taxation of passive investment income. The prescribed modifications include eliminating net operating loss carryovers and carrybacks, as well as any deductions allowable by §§ 241 to 247 and 249. §§ 1374(d)(2)(A)(ii) and 1375(b)(1)(B).

CHAPTER 10

FRINGE BENEFITS

In applying the provisions that deal with employee fringe benefits (including qualified deferred compensation plans), the same tax provisions that apply to partnerships and partners will apply to S corporations and to persons who own (or are deemed to own after applying § 318 stock attribution rules) more than two percent of an S corporation's outstanding stock or more than two percent of the total combined voting power of the corporation's stock. § 1372. Thus, there usually will be no difference in the tax treatment of fringe benefits whether a partnership form or Subchapter S form is utilized.

*

INDEX

References are to Pages

TAXATION OF—Cont'd
Built-in gain, 194–222
Passive investment income, 188–193

TERMINATION OF ELECTION
    Generally, 123–187
C short year, 177, 183–185
Cessation of qualification as S corporation, 124–175
New election after, 76, 176
New shareholder,
    Consent of, 173–174
Passive investment income, 185–187
Revocation, 173
S short year, 177, 183–185
Termination year, 176–185

TRUST
As a shareholder, 14, 29–30
    See, Shareholder, Permissible person
Electing Small Business Trust (ESBT), 35–37
Qualified Subchapter S Trust (QSST), 37–41, 125
Voting, 29–30

UNIFORM GIFT OR TRANSFERS TO MINORS ACT
See Stock, Nominal ownership

†